THE NEW
ALPHA

Be Three Times the Leader Through
Balance, Not Dominance

by
KENYADA MEADOWS

The New Alpha: Be Three Times the Leader Through Balance, Not Dominance

Written by Kenyada Meadows
Copyright © 2025 Kenyada Meadows

Design and cover art by Peaceful Profits.

Paperback ISBN: 978-1-967587-36-0
eBook ISBN: 978-1-967587-37-7

This book is dedicated to my parents who taught me the value of integrity, and that true strength begins with introspection, humility, and confident action. Your examples shaped not only my character, but my calling.

Table of Contents

Preface

A Critical Need

For most of human history, men have been typecast into, and have equally accepted, a role that prizes stoicism, dominance, and even brutality. They've been driven to demonstrate relentless performance in pursuit of never-ending victories. At the same time, the traditional role of man has blocked emotional signals, depth, and meaningful connection with others—even with themselves.

Boys have been conditioned to deny and divide their feelings, judging emotions in themselves and each other. Men now too often lead without sensitivity and vulnerability. They have been conditioned to support others even to the point of severe sacrifice, without truly supporting themselves in the most fundamental ways.

Leadership has been reduced to control, competition, and relentless displays of hardness. This process and lived reality has caused men to lose touch, not only with others, but with themselves, creating a terrible contradiction that men and the societies around them have been trying to reconcile with little real progress. The signs and problems have taken on different appearances over the centuries but remain fundamentally the same. Men have been dehumanized, stripped of normal emotions and outlets for those feelings, with mostly only anger remaining as an option. Worst of all, they keep doing it to themselves, deepening the damage.

I wrote this book to help men rename and reclaim their humanity. The word "human" is derived from the Latin word *homo*, meaning "man" and *humus* meaning "earth." This combination denotes that humans are beings of the Earth.

Earth holds countless materials, temperatures, and textures, each with its own feel. Men need to be brought back down to Earth, regrounded in what makes us all human. In addition, these Latin words provide a meaning that contrasts being of the Earth with being of the heavens. This further suggests that we are not perfect and don't have to be. In fact, we cannot be.

Meanwhile, society's view of men and their more-than-human strength run counter to the reality of imperfection. Men who want to change themselves and the world for the better must embrace receptivity and softness when required. The Earth does not receive new growth when the ground is hard, rigid, dark, and cold—and neither do people.

Some of the strongest substances on Earth are also the most flexible. For example, graphene is a two-dimensional sheet of carbon atoms arranged in a honeycomb shape and is known for being both incredibly strong and remarkably flexible. One of its uses is in body armor, which ironically symbolizes the very rigidity that keeps us stuck in old thinking. In other words, we often cling to the armor we think will protect us, but that same armor can become a prison, preventing us from growing and connecting. True strength, like that of graphene, comes from a balance of power and flexibility. It's in letting go of our most rigid defenses that we discover our capacity to bend, to adapt, and to grow in a way that nurtures growth in others too.

Water is another substance thought of as being incredibly strong, but in another way. Bruce Lee famously said, "Be water, my friend.[1]" This indicates adaptability, flexibility, and ability to flow. Few forces shape the Earth—and everything around them—more than flowing water.

But how do we "Be like water"? How do we blend strength with flexibility—filling spaces that need us without eroding them? How do we recognize and remember that men are human, have complex feelings, and are in need of social evolution? How do we grow beyond the old ways of defining strength? How do we become more emotionally present, more connected to ourselves and others, and more whole in our leadership and relationships?

At this point, we might wonder: Is it really feasible for softness and power to coexist, never mind lead to even greater strength than we have known so far? What is our real purpose and how do we live that combination with authenticity, and even tremendous impact? How do we make critical changes, and what do we change while still maintaining self-confidence and healthy masculinity? What will be our legacy? And can we build something lasting from something soft?

---

1   Bruce Lee, interview by Pierre Berton, *The Pierre Berton Show* (CBC Television, filmed December 9, 1971): 15:55, YouTube video, https://www.youtube.com/watch?v=ER5Z_MyUkJQ.

These are some of the very questions that I myself have struggled with. These questions have shaped my choices and compelled me to reimagine the meaning of manhood. That reimagining begins with finding balance in the three most critical spaces in our daily lives. The Three Pillars of the New Alpha address our most important relationships: at home, at work, and—perhaps most critically—with ourselves.

This book will not try to discard the notion that men have been, and can continue to be leaders; influential in how they behave, what they provide, and relentless in how they protect. This book will actually work to expand on how we can do all of that even better, while living full, balanced lives that also reward those around us, and those who come after us. It will help you feel less conflicted, more connected, and truly fulfilled.

–Kenyada Meadows

Introduction

But I would feel deep shame before the Trojans and the Trojan women with trailing gowns, if like a coward I were to shrink aside from the fighting. Nor does the spirit urge me on that way, for I have learned always to be brave and to fight in the front ranks of the Trojans, winning great glory for my father and for myself.
–HOMER, *Iliad*, Book 6

The Molding of Man

In the late 1800s, Auguste Rodin created one of the most famous and recognizable sculptures in history. It is of a man sitting in deep contemplation. Over time, *The Thinker* has taken on a universal significance related to philosophy and introspection. As you meditate on some of the ideas in this book, you may find yourself in a similar pose. This sculpture takes on an even deeper meaning to me than the meanings commonly described, because the sculpture is actually hollow.

Rodin used a wax casting method to create molds for his bronze works, which were hollow as a result. How ironic that one of the most recognizable symbols of thoughtfulness, depth, and a man, is actually empty inside. The men created by societies the world over and for all of human history, no matter their depth of responsibility, have generally been as hard and empty—hollowed out. Why do I make this claim?

Men have been robbed of their full humanity by being conditioned to reject their own emotional depth and sensitivity. They have been taught not to feel, acknowledge, or express most emotions, with the exception of anger and competitiveness, which then get exaggerated.

Men learn that showing too much tenderness or asking for help somehow threatens who they are or how they are supposed to exist.

Over time, this narrows our emotional range, cutting us off from essential parts of ourselves. Ironically, this weakening happens in the service of being strong. Much of what we've been taught to see as strength is actually a form of restriction. Like a corset, machismo squeezes men into a shape that looks impressive on the outside, but leaves little room to breathe or to really be themselves, especially in their own way.

We create this mold of a man by carving out the inside. We deaden the vulnerability, the uncertainty, and the emotional nuances men, as humans, were made to experience. Then, after starving these essential aspects from a man's youth, even in their influential formative years when they require them most, we throw the now hardened men into partnerships, parenting, and other leadership roles. These all demand sensitivity, empathy, and inclusivity we've previously attempted to strip from them.

That contradiction between what we've been trained to suppress and what we're expected to be—and ironically includes some of what we've suppressed—creates dissonance. This dissonance and frustration shows up everywhere: in poor communication at home, in broken relationships, and in burnout. In men, it shows up as violence, as criminal activity, as addiction, and as death by suicide[2] at rates so high we should be asking where this pain is coming from. And not just asking, but working fervently to address the causes of this pain.

Placing blame for these problems is futile and not really possible. Instead, we should capitalize on our new found and ever growing awareness. Most of us were never given the tools to effectively navigate this topic. How do we process anger without exploding or imploding? Without shutting down? How do we communicate emotions without feeling weak? Without being seen as weak? How do we model tenderness for our children and compassion for others without fearing that we'll lose their respect? How often have men even considered these questions, much less attempted to answer them?

The cost of disconnection isn't just personal; it's generational. When men are only expected to lead through strength, control, or performance, we end up with one-dimensional leadership: appearing capable on the outside, but emotionally absent underneath. Our sons inherit suppression and depression, while our daughters learn broken and incomplete expectations from the men in their lives. This cycle will continue, unless we choose to break it.

---

2   "Suicide Data and Statistics," *Centers for Disease Control and Prevention*, last reviewed November 9, 2023, https://www.cdc.gov/suicide/facts/data.html.

We can't change what we don't acknowledge. But once our eyes are opened and we really see how these generational issues present themselves, the next step is to ask: How do we begin to live differently, certainly for our own sake, but also to leave a better and richer legacy? For me that shift started with hope and, very simply, with the way I choose to focus my thoughts.

The Power of Horizontal Thinking

In my professional life, I've been trained to think horizontally, that is to look across topics, issues, themes, teams, and disciplines to find connections. In business we don't just stay in our lane; we pull from what works in one area and apply it to another. We talk about best practices, transferable insights, and alignment across functions. Synthesis is a critical part of any analysis. But for a long time, I wasn't applying that same kind of thinking broadly, and certainly not at home or related to my self-care or personal considerations. But why not?

At work I benefited from clear goals, clear processes, ongoing feedback systems, coaching, and formal and timely performance evaluations. The relationship between actions, outcomes, and rewards was linear. I participated in established processes and frameworks at work intended to create and maintain order, while I facilitated excellence. These were all things that helped me contribute meaningfully, grow, and lead better. But I wasn't bringing that same intentionality into the other key parts of my life. I wasn't asking myself:

- What does excellence look like here? What is required to achieve it?

- What's the system for growth, support, or even repair when problems arise?
- How can I be productive and optimize rewards in these other critical areas of my life?
- How should these goals all be defined and measured?

As humans, we tend to compartmentalize the versions of who we are: This is who I am at work, this is who I am at home, and this is who I am with and to myself. While this makes sense given the differences in contexts and requirements, we are still fundamentally the same and carry all the people and places with us. The reason this often happens is that in some ways we feel we can take a break from one environment or group of people when in another space. But our lives, moods, and outlooks are not so modular or detachable. Our various roles blend, even bleed into each other. The frustration from work comes home. The disconnection, loneliness, and self-doubt seep into how we parent and lead. The silence in our relationships reverberates and echoes elsewhere. We are whole beings in need of whole solutions. This also means that we have rich opportunities.

Thinking horizontally is about observation and integration, engaging the otherwise separate areas of life that actually need to be in conversation and partnership with one another. If we can develop leadership principles for the office, we can also develop relationship principles for our homes. If we can commit to strategy and vision in our careers, we can do the same for how we raise our children, support our partners, and nurture ourselves. We can ensure balance in the way we discipline and reward ourselves and in the way we speak to ourselves. The shift comes when we apply balance to all areas of life, not just to the elements within areas that feel the most productive, or even where we spend the most time. The goal is not to lead or dominate in only one area of life. What if we could be excellent—and *truly* excel—in all areas of life: at work, at home, and within ourselves.

The Three Pillars of the New Alpha

This book was written to share my own reflections and journey in enhancing the three most important relationships in the three most important areas of my life. We will focus on our relationships at **home**, at **work**, and **with ourselves** (arguably the most critical of them all). These are what I call the Three Pillars of the New Alpha, a model of leadership that isn't driven by dominance, but by balance. The New Alpha leads with presence, not performance. He prioritizes wholeness over hustle. He understands that real strength comes from integrating all parts of himself and not just the parts that earn praise, power, or a paycheck.

These areas of life are not silos or roles to switch on and off depending on the day or time. They are environments we move through every day, physically and mentally. How we show up in one inevitably affects how we show up in the others.

For many men, **work** usually gets most of the attention because it's where we're trained to strive and perform, compete and compare, where structure exists, and where we most often measure our value as providers. And we are not alone in this evaluation of our performance, abilities, and outcomes. The world appears to be watching—people both near and far.

Home often comes second and it's where we give what's left after the workday ends. After all, isn't this what and who we're doing it all for? Sometimes we are present; other times, it means distance. Sometimes, we carry the frustrations and even the competitiveness and rigidity of our jobs into our interactions with our partners and children. But the way we're expected to lead at work doesn't always translate at home. The dynamics are different. The expectations are different. Our families aren't coworkers, and our homes aren't extensions of the office. When we blur those lines, connection suffers. We may wonder why our families don't appreciate or even understand all we do for them—all we *have* to do—often at great and unspoken sacrifice. The simple truth, which we'll explore more in these pages, is that our families don't want to be relegated to being second after work, and understandably so.

And then there's the Self, the part so fundamental and close to us that we sometimes even forget it's there—that we are there. The self is the part that most often gets left behind or ignored, especially for men, even though it's always there. This is the first thing we mute, override, or sacrifice when any of the areas are in conflict, even if it gets too loud and seems to be in need. We often try to numb what hasn't already been deadened. When this part of us is out of balance, we can usually feel it but can't always name it because the Self has been conditioned to endure. Never complain, never explain.

This book is about the ways of restoring balance between and within these three pillars and the related benefits of doing so. It aims to help develop deeper awareness, intention, and alignment so that you can live a life that opens all the doors of who you are and not close off the parts that feel too vulnerable to show. It also aims to help calibrate and evaluate how we measure our performance and ourselves. A man who is grounded within himself, connected at home, and confident in how he participates and leads at work, creates a ripple effect that is sustainable and transforms more than his own life. In fact, this is how he builds a legacy that extends beyond his work in a healthy and truly constructive way.

Many of us aren't there yet. The truth is, too many men are struggling to find that balance. Even good intentions can get twisted when we're operating from outdated models. Men who don't have balance in these three areas face persistent undercurrents of loneliness, emptiness, anger, and dissatisfaction. In the **home**, imbalance often shows up as divorce, emotional distance, or chronic discord. At **work**, it shows up in dysfunctional teams, unhealthy competition, office politics, malignant leadership, and burnout. In the **self**, it often takes the form of drug use, abuses of food or drink, too little sleep, loneliness, depression, and even suicide.

We're taught to function, to deliver, and that as men we ought to be able to hold everything together. But very few of us have the spaces or the language to name what we're feeling, let alone process and effectively manage why we're feeling those ways. Even in friendships, men often don't feel able to discuss these things without fear of judgment or misunderstanding.

However, what I have found is that once these topics are brought up, men do want to open up. They speak and listen keenly. They just need to feel that they have permission, the right tools, and a safe space. That's why I wrote this book. It's here to provide that language, those tools, and that space. It will offer frameworks for reflection to help you find balance, however you define balance in your life.

Strength and Vulnerability Are Not Opposites

A big part of this work is recognizing that strength and vulnerability are not on opposite ends of the spectrum. We've been taught to believe that in order to be strong, we have to shut down our emotions, push through what we really feel, and stay guarded against the world. But that's not real strength, it's conditioning. It's the narrow script that fails to represent what it really means to be fully human.

For a long time, I bought into that programming. I went to therapy for several years before I ever told anyone, besides my partner and my mother, that I was going. Some of my closest friends never knew. The truth is, I used to be judgmental about therapy. I remember when I first moved to New York, it seemed to me like everyone I went out with or spoke to talked about their therapist. I remember wondering at that time if having a therapist was just a way to be in vogue or flaunt a status symbol.

But when I started going myself, I realized therapy isn't about fixing something broken. It is about developing the tools to slow down, process what I was thinking and feeling, and lead with more awareness and openness. It helped me put my thoughts into words and my feelings into perspective. It gave me new ideas and allowed me to tap into a source of wisdom that was within me—wisdom that is within us all. Through the conversations, questions, and questioning of assumptions that are often treated as foregone conclusions, I was able to think more freely, clearly, and in some ways simply. Therapy provided me the space to be honest with myself and to learn more about who I am. It made the need to modify and enhance myself much more clear, and it opened up new pathways to do so.

Recognizing and leveraging vulnerability requires strength and is a precursor to more strengthening. Vulnerabilities may be soft spots, but not all soft spots are weaknesses, especially when they lead to transformation and resolve. When a bone is broken and then heals, that point of former vulnerability becomes slightly thicker and more dense than it was before. In other words, stronger. In addressing those tender places with structure and intention, a different kind of strength is built—the kind that includes vulnerability as an essential part of the process, instead of hiding and denying it. Leaders appreciate that vulnerability is not only a chance for healing, but connection. People want to know that you know what they are experiencing, that you can relate, and that you are as human as they are. Vulnerability is what opens the door to change and deepens our connection with our partners, our children, and our teams.

Men too often fail to create or accept invitations to cross these bridges and points of connection. While I sometimes use and enjoy the imagery of the expression, "May the bridges we burn light the way," I also recognize a cynical and macho tendency in the words that holds a certain gravity that is attractive to men and pulls us in. We are more inclined to destroy than to find or create safe spaces to practice vulnerability. These spaces have thus far been missing, or are so few and far between as to be easily missed. And who recognized that there was a need? Men have been missing some critical aspects of community, because they have been missing such critical aspects of themselves.

That is where you and I, as well as this book come in. The burning is done. Let the building begin.

Leadership Begins With the Self

If you take one thing away from reading this book, I hope it is this: Leadership begins with and inside you—within the self.

One of the biggest realizations I've had is that leadership often begins in places and moments of weakness and uncertainty, when things are unfamiliar. I learned this through therapy, fatherhood, becoming an executive coach, and receiving coaching. Even the way leadership is defined is often too narrow, too loud, or too sure.

The static and stale versions of leadership many of us were taught involve control and a surefooted appearance. But I've come to believe, and we'll continue to explore in this book, that authentic leadership is about what we do and how we are *when* we are uncertain and wounded. It's about getting up and showing up as our true imperfect, sometimes scared, selves but still taking ownership. This is where we take and model responsibility. Balanced leadership also requires our willingness to say, "I don't know," or "I was wrong," or "I need help," "I'm going to," or "We're going to fix it, together." That kind of leadership isn't built overnight. It takes reflection, intention, and the right tools to begin the journey. That is what this book aims to share with you.

How to Use This Book

This book aims to offer guidance that helps men reconnect with our true human nature, to challenge the stories we've inherited, and to offer a framework for living with more balance, intention, and depth.

But this book isn't only written with the man in mind. It's also here for women—women who are raising boys, working with men, or trying to understand masculinity differently. It's for the partners, spouses, and loved ones of men, employers and organizational leaders who lead men, and for anyone doing the work of becoming more whole humans.

Throughout this book, you'll find personal reflections, examples from men's lives, and questions designed to help you pause and take inventory of what you're feeling and how you're responding to those emotions. None of this is about perfection. It's about getting honest and giving yourself the space to grow into a version of masculinity that aligns with who you truly are, not just what the world expects you to be.

I'll guide you through exploring how we tend to show up at home, work, and for ourselves, what gets in the way, and what's possible when we lead from a place of being whole instead of feeling like we're giving a performance. At the end of the book, you'll find exercises that can support you in applying these principles in your relationships, your routines, your leadership, and your legacy.

There's no single path forward. But there is a common thread: You have to be willing to reflect, to take action, and to challenge what you've always assumed was true.

So as you read, I invite you to:

- **Engage** with the questions, not just as mental exercises but as personal check-ins.
- **Reflect** on what you've inherited, what you've internalized, and what you're ready to release.
- **Take action** in your everyday life with your partner, your children, your colleagues, and yourself.
- **Join the conversation** with other men who are doing this work too.
- **Stay open** to what becomes possible when we stop performing and start leading from a place of presence.

So if you're ready to lead differently and change the way you show up for yourself, your work, and your family, let's get started.

Part 1
Foundations

Chapter 1

The Making of Men

*Man...still bears in his bodily frame the indelible
stamp of his lowly origin.*
–CHARLES DARWIN, *The Descent of Man*, 1871

The Origins of Masculine Expectations

When we talk about gender roles today, such as who leads, who nurtures, who provides, and how, we often forget how far back the blueprint goes. It actually goes back to the very beginning of time.

Historically, men hunted and women often nurtured. Why? Because men, generally larger, faster, and stronger, took on the strenuous and often dangerous task of catching food that did not want to be caught. They also had the responsibility of protecting the group from predators or outside threats if there was to be any hope at all for survival. Meanwhile, women often did work of a more domestic nature, things that did not require as much strength or would take them too far away from the home.

Women carried and birthed children, breastfed them, and remained physically tethered to their young in ways that not only facilitated nourishment, but fostered intimacy. That intimacy was born of hours of daily care, feeding, and presence with their children. The maternal bond was instinctive on many levels, even binding the child to its mother by her smell. As a result, women naturally became the center of the early domestic environment with child-rearing responsibilities. They shaped the emotional and cultural rhythms of the household while also managing critical tasks like gathering nuts and berries, cooking, and maintaining otherwise safe and relatively comfortable living conditions.

These roles for men and women evolved from necessity, not ideology, creating a framework that has persisted across the globe and through history based on its practical origin and resulting applications. Eventually, these necessary roles gave rise to cultural patterns, which evolved into expectations, and then social norms that have endured for millennia.

Examples of this framework's historical acceptance and continued relevance can be found in many East Asian cultures, particularly those of the Chinese, where it is extremely common to see sculptures and motifs of Fu Lions or Imperial Guardian Lions in architecture and design. The male lion is traditionally depicted with a ball or globe under his paw, protecting the structure in front of which he is placed, symbolizing power, dominance, and protection in the external world.

The female lion, on the other hand, and at his side, is shown with a cub under her paw, representing nurturing, protection of those within, and the continuity of life. The pair were traditionally placed at the entrances of palaces, temples, and wealthy homes to ward off evil spirits and to convey strength and protection. They also, no doubt reinforced gender-based expectations.

These symbols, carved in stone, were reflections of deeply held beliefs about who men and women were supposed to be. And while the tools and settings have changed, the roles they represent have proven remarkably persistent.

Following the Scripts

Although the ways people live and contribute to society have changed over time, our gender-based traditions and thinking have endured through to the present day. So what happens when our environments evolve and survival is no longer dependent on physical strength, or when our cultural expectations are no longer aligned with these traditions? Are these traditions actually even bad? And have we come to a point where they no longer serve us?

That's the tension we're living with today: Our lives have evolved, but the expectations haven't. On the surface, especially in the developed world, things have shifted. But under that surface, humankind is still largely operating from those millennia-old scripts shaped by that early arrangement. These continue to define what it means to be a man and how men are supposed to show up at work, at home, and within themselves.

We see these scripts in the media we grew up on: action heroes who win by physical strength and grit, dads who stay emotionally distant, leaders who never ask for help. We saw them in our fathers, our coaches, and our mentors. We see them in our brothers, and our sons. They didn't always shout the following words, or even say them out loud, but we learned them just the same: Be tough, steady, and in control. Be a man!

The word *alpha* originates from the Greek alphabet where *alpha* is the first letter. Over time, *alpha* has come to symbolize "first" or "primary," denoting hierarchy. It began to be used this way especially in the study of animal behavior. The term continued to evolve and was popularized to describe the dominant individual in a social group. From there, it evolved into popular psychology and leadership language with references to "alpha males" and "alpha leaders," which denote someone perceived as strong, steady, and dominant—someone *in charge.*

While this classic (read: old) model of the alpha male has its place and has undoubtedly been useful, even essential; it has also been destructive and in some key ways has become critically outdated. These scripts should no longer be broadly and mindlessly applied, nor assumed as they have been in the past. Why? Because some of the assumptions and perceived benefits were never true in the first place. They have become increasingly less true as we learn more about what really works and endures. We keep subscribing to them, often without realizing the cost of embracing these assumptions.

That's why this book is about redefining what leadership means in the modern world. The New Alpha isn't the loudest voice in the room, taking up space with mustered bravado and jumping at the chance to prove his worth. He leads with equilibrium across the three pillars of life: **self**, **home**, and **work**. He knows that leadership starts within, and he takes responsibility for how he shows up—in his relationships and decisions. The New Alpha is emotionally aware, grounded in purpose, and committed to growth.

Evolving Beyond Old Definitions

Have we been shaped into men who feel at odds with masculinity itself? Have we inherited a version of manhood that doesn't match our values or our desires? One that looks successful from the outside, but leaves many men wondering: *Is this really what it takes to lead and succeed? Is this really all there is after all I've done? Is this what I want for other men, society, myself, or my son?*

I'll be direct in telling you: No! There is more, there is better, and there is another way. A way to feel and be human, and not just to survive, but to work toward greater, lasting fulfillment. There will be more clarity, more connection, more feeling, and more confidence with a stronger sense of purpose and peace.

But you will not find those things by doing more of the same, by being stoic and unchanging. You won't find those benefits unless you work to balance your life across and within the three pillars of the self, home, and work. You will find those results when you ask and deeply consider better questions—by reflecting candidly on who you are, what you have done, who you have become, and how you want to be. By reflecting on how you impact other people. With some simple adjustments and commitment, you can build and reshape a life that reflects who you are and what you value at your core.

This book is an invitation to examine these questions with honesty and humility, to challenge yourself and the men you care about to begin reframing what manhood, leadership, and relationships could look like at their most optimal. This will not be based on antiquated, somehow deficient scripts, but based on the kind of enriched life we can sketch with fresh ink and a new pen.

In the next chapter, we'll explore how these scripts show up in our lives today and how they shape who we become.

Chapter 2

The Disconnected Man

Most men lead lives of quiet desperation and go to the grave with the song still in them.
–Henry David Thoreau

The Conversation That Changed My Perspective

A few years ago, McKinsey—a global management consulting firm that conducts research on various business topics—ran a study on paternity leave. The findings weren't exactly shocking, but they were sobering. They found that while many companies now offer paternity leave, a staggering number of fathers don't take the full amount of time offered to them.[3] Some don't take any because they're afraid of what it might cost them at work.

According to the study, less than half of new fathers who were offered parental leave took it, while 20% of the men who did

---

3   McKinsey & Company, "A Fresh Look at Paternity Leave: Why the Benefits Extend Beyond the Personal," *McKinsey & Company*, June 29, 2023. https://www.mckinsey.com/capabilities/people-and-organizational-performance/our-insights/a-fresh-look-at-paternity-leave-why-the-benefits-extend-beyond-the-personal.

were afraid their leave would negatively impact their careers. They feared missing out on promotions, being seen as less committed, or losing momentum at work.

In many organizations, especially ones that are male-dominated or that have high-performance cultures, taking paternity leave isn't normalized. Fathers worry about being judged by peers or supervisors for taking time off to prioritize family, creating pressure for men to "check in" or keep working during leave to prove their dedication. Without explicit support from leadership, men may feel hesitant or guilty for taking the full amount of time off.

I was one of these men who almost didn't take paternity leave for these same reasons. It wasn't that I didn't value family or believe in bonding with my newborn daughter, but somewhere along the way, I had internalized a belief that rest was optional. I believed that as a man with the hunger to succeed, I needed to keep moving and keep proving my worth.

My company offers a generous leave policy for parents, one I'd always respected. But I never imagined actually using it myself. I assumed that kind of time off was for people who were junior enough in their responsibilities or already had their trust fund all figured out. Maybe they had arrived at whatever level they intended to achieve at the firm or they weren't that far off and were in no particular rush to get to where they wanted to go.

But I didn't have a trust fund. I had ambitions, and I had a desire to live up to my full potential. I worried that taking time away would make me invisible: It was too risky in a competitive environment. Why should I expect to be given more responsibility and to get better recognition—in other words, move up in my career—if I was absent for months out of the year?

Being gone doesn't only impact the period of time you aren't in the office. There may be multiyear projects or other high-profile undertakings that could just as easily go to someone else in your absence. Someone who will be there for the ramp-up and the kickoff, who will move things along while you're gone, but who will provide consistency even after you come back. And all of that could have been yours if you simply hadn't left.

The irony is I've always supported the idea of family leave for everyone else. But when it came to applying that idea to myself, I hit a wall of unspoken rules and internal resistance. Even though I knew better intellectually, there was a voice in my head telling me fathers don't need that time in the same way as mothers. We didn't carry the baby or go through the trauma of birth. We're there to help, to do the diaper changes and grocery runs and check-ins. But is that worth disappearing from work to do?

So I took two weeks off at the time of my daughter's birth, but I didn't take the full leave. After the two weeks, I went back to the office. I thought I could balance my new home life and career without making any real adjustments based on what it meant to have a newborn. What I ended up doing was burning the candle at both ends without realizing it until one phone call changed everything.

One Thursday evening I was catching up with a former manager, let's call her Mary, whom I admire deeply: not only for her work ethic, but for how she navigated pressure with grace. I shared the news that my daughter had been born. She was surprised because, while I had taken two weeks of vacation earlier that year, she knew I hadn't used any meaningful portion of my firm's generous benefit related to family leave.

Then it was my turn to be surprised as Mary strongly encouraged me to take the time. All of it. She acted as a sounding board for some of my honest concerns as I explained why I hadn't taken the leave already.

I recall that when I hung up at the end of that conversation, I felt a weight come off my shoulders that I hadn't even known was there before. As I stood up, I felt lifted up. It suddenly felt realistic for me to step away, use my family leave, and still move forward in my career.

The phone call with Mary showed me an example of true leadership. A great leader reminds you of who you are and who you *want* to become. I had been reminded that a career is a long game, that self-care was critical, and that life outside of the professional world really matters. These were truths I knew intellectually and that conversation helped me internalize them.

In the McKinsey study I mentioned earlier, 100% of the fathers who took time off were interviewed and said they were glad they did. Even those who felt it might hurt their careers still said they'd take the leave again. The benefits of paternity leave show why. That shared experience builds a stronger family bond between the parents. It also changes the way fathers show up for their kids. That early time isn't just memorable for dad;

it's formative for the baby. When dads are hands-on from the beginning, they tend to stay engaged long after the diapers and midnight feedings are over. They build lasting connections, not only with their child, but with their role as a parent.

The impact goes beyond home life, bleeding into other areas. Taking family leave can make it easier for a partner to return to work sooner, which means the family's financial future doesn't rest on one person's shoulders. It's one way we start to chip away at the wage gap and open more choices for both parents.

Even in the workplace, the benefits are clear. Fathers who take leave often return with more loyalty, more appreciation, and more energy for their careers. When people feel seen and supported during the most meaningful moments of their lives, they tend to bring more of themselves when they return to work.

Looking back, that decision to take an extended leave wasn't only about my family. It was the moment I began to understand what it meant to rebalance the three pillars that hold a man's life: self, home, and work.

Up to that point, I had overfed the work pillar while starving the others. I told myself I was doing it for my family, all while slowly disconnecting from both them and myself. But stepping away, even briefly, gave me clarity. I realized I had been cannibalizing my own well-being and emotional presence in service of a version of success that couldn't sustain me. I had been feeding the illusion of achievement while starving the parts of myself that make life worth living.

The Hollow Man

That phone call was a wake-up call to my humanity. Despite my support of parental leave, until I became a father myself, I hadn't fully grasped the emotional, physical, and relational demands that come with caring for a child. As I changed diapers and spent afternoons walking my newborn daughter around the neighborhood, I began to confront a deeper truth, one that I think many men live with but rarely articulate. And because my leave happened during a time when much of the world had slowed down—when people were working from home, grounded, and no longer traveling—that truth came into even sharper focus.

Throughout time, men have been framed up and hollowed out. We're built to be strong, but as the world redefined masculinity, something vital got cut out of us. We lost the parts that made us wholly human: the softer side of masculinity that act as counterweights to our strength. These aspects, like vulnerability and emotional intelligence, are essential. Without them, we're incomplete.

Because of this evolution, many modern men fall into a category I call The Hollow Man.

On the outside, he looks like he has it all together. He's got a good job, a steady paycheck, a nice home, and a family he deeply loves. But on the inside, there's a void. He feels a dullness, a quiet ache he can't quite name. Somewhere along the way, he was taught not to show that something is missing. Maybe he doesn't even acknowledge that he feels it. It's a hole in a person that's there, but that others often can't see. It may be all that person sees, and exactly what everyone else sees through. It may be all that person tries to fill, but that everyone else walks through.

You can see it in the dad who never misses work but hasn't tucked his kid into bed in months. You hear it in the high-performer who runs marathons and does million-dollar deals but feels numb inside. It's in the man who checks all the boxes society says he should and still lies awake at night wondering if those boxes are all there is to life.

We've been conditioned to define success by what we produce. We've been taught to chase milestones like career promotions, financial security, home ownership, a spouse, two kids, and a dog. All this while silencing any part of us that questions whether those things are truly fulfilling.

I know that man because I've been that man. For years I tried to feed the hollowness by steadily giving myself a diet of accomplishments—academic degrees, career achievements, stamps in my passport. I sought enrichment through personal growth and worldly experience, believing that if I just did more, achieved more, or traveled farther that I would eventually feel whole. But no matter how many external markers I collected, the internal emptiness remained.

The idea of manhood has been squeezed into a definition so narrow that it has created four distinct problems that contribute to forming the hollow man.

Problem #1: We've been boxed into rigid masculine norms.
From an early age, we're taught not only *what* to be, but *how* to appear: stoic, composed, and always in control. The problem

isn't just that this approach is limiting. It's that it starts to feel like a performance. We're told to show up like a superhero, but inside we're exhausted, disconnected, and unsure if we're allowed to feel anything at all.

Problem #2: We've become emotionally disconnected.

That pressure to "man up" doesn't only harden our exterior; it numbs us inside. We lose access to our own emotions. We've learned to mute them. Over time, that disconnection becomes a barrier. It shows up in our relationships and in the way we move through the world. We're physically, even mentally, present but emotionally distant. And that takes a toll, both on ourselves and on the people we care about most.

Problem #3: We've been conditioned to normalize destructive behavior.

In a culture that rewards control, aggression, and unchecked ambition, it's easy for harmful behaviors to get dressed up as leadership. We start to think that working ourselves into the ground, staying silent through stress, or burying our pain is part of being a man. Historically, some have called this "toxic masculinity." I won't use that phrase in this book because I want this conversation to feel like an invitation, not an accusation, but it's important to acknowledge that this behavior is destructive.

These damaging patterns don't make us stronger, they make us brittle. Brittle things don't bend, they snap. An eggshell shows this clearly. Its dome shape makes it remarkably strong under balanced pressure—you can squeeze it end to end with surprising force without breaking it. But apply pressure unevenly, and even a fingernail can shatter it. Men are much the same: We can endure enormous stress when it's distributed across the right supports, but will collapse quickly when the weight is concentrated in one place.

To use another example, consider the human eye. On the outside, the sclera is tough and surprisingly resistant to puncture, but a blunt strike can rupture delicate inner structures and fracture the bones around it. Like the egg, the eye's resilience and fragility are able to withstand some forces, but are undone by others. That's the paradox of the hollow man: We look durable, yet under the wrong kind of pressure, we break. And when we do, the break is rarely contained. These destructive patterns spill into marriages, workplaces, friendships, and fatherhood. They cause our relationships to crumble. They encourage us to form addictions to things like alcohol, work, porn, scrolling, or anything that helps us avoid sitting still with ourselves. We look for anything that numbs the ache.

Problem #4: We've lost touch with our humanity.

As men, we've been taught to value dominance, leadership, and restraint. We've carved out the emotional parts of ourselves to fit the mold. And then we wonder why we feel disconnected, why relationships feel distant, and why rest feels unsafe. We've spent so much time becoming the version of a man that's acceptable to the world that we've forgotten what it feels like to be human.

It's time to examine how this disconnection shapes our relationship with power, and what it would take to reclaim it on our own terms.

Redefining Man's Relationship With Power and Fear

This hollowness not only affects how we feel, it shapes how we lead. And nowhere is that more evident than in how we've come to define power.

We've been conditioned to be powerful. That's the idea, right? Be the protector, the leader, the one in control.

Power, for most of us, was handed down as a script. One that said: don't show your hand, don't reveal too much, and don't be vulnerable. Just keep moving. Keep performing and keep proving. From a young age, we were told that power looked like dominance, decisiveness, and assertiveness. In the absence of those traits, you simply weren't a real man. So we followed the script, taking the lead, even when we lacked clarity or connection to our own feelings.

The irony of all this is that while we've been trained to chase power, most of us were never taught how to own it. At least not in a way that creates connection or nourishes trust. What if we consider, for a moment, that the traditional idea of masculine power isn't a strength but a weakness?

I was reminded of this during a communication training I attended a few years ago. It was about how to be a more effective speaker, how to read the room, and how to tailor your message. As I sat there, listening to strategies about massaging your message and managing perception, I couldn't help but feel how exhausting all of those suggestions felt.

I've spent most of my adult life assuming that if we're mature enough, serious enough, and committed enough to the goal—

whether in business or in life—then we shouldn't have to twist or spin the way we talk. We should be able to be honest. For me transparency is respect, and respect is power. If I'm giving you the full picture, clear, complete, and unvarnished, then I'm giving you something far more valuable than direction. I'm giving you a choice. I'm allowing you to operate with full agency. So when I feel like someone is being evasive, when I sense manipulation, when key information is being withheld, I take it personally. It disrupts trust, and without trust, there is no connection.

But I've also learned this: Sometimes people don't withhold information because they want power. They do it because they're afraid.

Your kid lies to you because they're scared of being punished. Your colleague spins a story because they're afraid of looking weak. We all do this. Maybe you downplay your own stress, guilt, or grief because somewhere deep down, you're scared of how it will be received.

Whether we acknowledge it or not, fear shapes how we use our power. And when fear is in the driver's seat, power, like the hollow man, becomes brittle. This fear-based power fractures relationships, it keeps people guessing, and worst of all, it keeps us alone.

So what happens if we flip the script? What if we started treating vulnerability as part of our power, not a threat to it? When we break through the typecast of masculinity, we begin to star in a script that is written and directed by us.

Despite what society might have told us about vulnerability, it's not a sign of weakness. Vulnerability does not diminish our power. When we admit we're not okay, when we ask for help, when we allow someone else to really see us, we build relational connections. Real power is not the guy who has all the answers. (Who does?) It's the one who can sit across from his partner or his team or his child and say, "I don't know yet, but I'm listening." That's the kind of power that creates lasting influence in the home, office, and within ourselves.

Re-Parenting Yourself

If redefining power begins with honesty and vulnerability, then it also demands a deep commitment to self-directed growth—an internal responsibility that cannot be outsourced. As a man, even as a boy, how many things did you teach yourself? How many things did you experiment with to figure out how it worked or how to use it best or how to do it best?

When I was in college, the first time I drove a standard shift car, it was a little navy blue vehicle belonging to my friend Shane. The second time was a little white car belonging to my buddy Dexter. Both times were in parking lots. The third time I drove a stick was right after I bought a six-speed Honda Accord coupe with a VTEC engine. I was an hour north of Denver on a Friday afternoon during rush hour. Before I left the lot, I read some Google articles on when to shift, mostly based on the car's speed in miles per hour. I also quickly learned how the engine sounds when it's pleading. I made it home after stalling only once. I played no music, there was no phone, no company in the passenger seat; it was just me listening to and feeling out my car in stop-and-go traffic on the highway for over an hour.

When I was in high school, during a short class period when Mrs. Pierce knew that we'd soon be going to a special assembly, and it didn't make sense for her to start her math lesson, she granted the boys permission to play chess. We agreed to do so quietly and gathered round the single board in our possession at the time. Damien and Franklyn started playing and I asked them if they could explain why they were moving certain pieces the way they were. I think it was Damien, still a good friend to this day, who said "I don't really feel like teaching anybody how to play chess today." Franklyn agreed. We were in our early teens and they weren't intending at all to be mean. I said nothing, but I forgot nothing. That very weekend I asked my mother to take me to buy a chessboard. We actually bought two—one was a smaller magnetic travel set that I could study in the car.

You also have stories like this I'm sure. You've seen countless opportunities to know something, so you learned it. You knew that there were advantages even if you didn't know or couldn't even imagine what they all were. The fact that your parents or others didn't teach you a full range of communication, or how to manage your anger or how to feel and acknowledge your own emotions, is no excuse. You're a man now. You're an adult now. You have to re-parent yourself. Now. The balance is yours to pursue and preserve. It's no longer anyone else's responsibility. But your responsibility now extends further and much beyond this. You now know what others around you need to know, and in this book we will discuss how you can influence and lead them more effectively.

What You Can Expect Within These Pages

I didn't know it at the time, but taking that paternity leave was my first real step toward living the life I'm describing in this book. Not a life free of pressure or responsibility, but one where presence, purpose, and power can finally coexist in all three pillars of life.

What you'll find in the pages ahead isn't a list of to-dos or some empty motivational speech. It's an invitation to reconnect with what makes you whole. It's about shifting the way you relate to yourself, your family, your work, and your identity as a man. Because no matter where you're starting from, you can lead a life that feels more honest and more aligned with your values, your purpose, and your relationships.

Here's what you can expect when you begin to engage with the ideas and practices shared throughout this book:

- You'll start to move through life with greater clarity and self-awareness, not just reacting to pressure, but intentionally responding to what really matters.
- You'll build stronger relationships with your partner, your children, and your colleagues because you'll be showing up more fully with emotional presence and a willingness to be seen.
- You'll learn how to create healthy boundaries at work and at home, so you can give your best without running down to empty.

- You'll develop a version of leadership that's not based on control or performance, but on trust, transparency, and real connection.
- And most importantly, you'll begin to feel a deeper sense of alignment between who you are and how you show up.

This journey is about returning to your full humanity, not only the parts the world rewards, but also the parts you've had to silence in order to survive. It's about living in a way that doesn't require you to choose between being strong and being vulnerable, providing and being present, or achieving and being alive.

So as you turn the page, I invite you to be honest, be curious, and be open to what might shift as you invite these concepts into your life.

Chapter 3

Success at the Expense of the Self

The unexamined life is not worth living.
–SOCRATES

The Pressure Beneath the Surface

Most of us are living a kind of double life, one that on the outside looks composed and competent, and on the inside feels like the pressures we face are building toward an inevitable explosion. There's the version of ourselves the world sees: capable, composed, dependable. We go to work, show up for our families, and knock out the to-do list. We say the right things, keep our cool, and stay in motion.

The result of these two contrasting views is like condensation on a cold can. On the outside, everything looks fine. But inside, the temperature is rising. When the difference between an internal climate and an external environment becomes too great, pressure builds. If we don't slow down long enough to address that tension, it eventually leads to a rupture. The can bursts open and everything that was inside escapes into the outer world.

For some men, that rupture looks like burnout. Maybe you're pouring everything into your job while your family fades into the background. Or you experience the opposite: giving everything to everyone else at home while neglecting yourself until the body gives out, or the mind begins to fray.

Sometimes this tension will cause people to escalate into substance abuse, emotional or physical violence, road rage, or the mistreatment of people one doesn't even know. Other times it's more subtle and harder for the outside world to see, manifesting as depression, disconnection, malaise, or a chronic, low-grade unhappiness that doesn't have a clear name but refuses to go away.

It could ultimately be nothing as tense as any of those things but simply an unfulfilled, unlived life. It could appear as a silent resignation, a slow drifting away from your own potential. The days blur and the dreams shrink as you begin to live a life devoid of introspection or self-reflection, a life that isn't lived on purpose. It might look like giving up on the people and practices that light you up. Or you may start settling, like staying in a job that drains you or a relationship that no longer reflects who you are. You just keep going with the flow without ever asking whether that flow is taking you anywhere you actually want to go.

As Socrates famously said, "The unexamined life is not worth living." And while that may be a bit of a stretch, there's truth in it. A life without reflection—both personal and relational—can feel like a slow extinction.

The Conditioning of Manhood

So, as men, how did we get here? It's not as if we arrived at this place overnight. It happened gradually, almost imperceptibly. We got here through subtly adapting our behavior over the course of our lifetimes based on messages we've received from our parents, our mentors, our community, and society at large about what it looks like to be a successful man.

When I was a boy, my father urged me to always be the best. It was a message rooted in love and protection. But at times this message promoted competition over collaboration and results over relationships.

My father thought he was doing the right thing. He was passing down messages his father had taught him and what his father's father had taught before, shaped by our Caribbean culture and his own hopes for me to excavate and refine my gifts. By pushing me to be the best, he was preparing me not only for success, but to withstand future challenges.

Logically then, I would measure my worth by how well I performed. And many men approach life the same way based on what the men around them have said to them about what it means to succeed in life.

By always striving to be the best, rivalry became a key component in my understanding of what it meant to be a man. As men, we're conditioned to compete with each other, with ourselves, and with the world around us.

Competition shows up everywhere, telling us to: be faster, last longer, do more. Being better becomes more than a goal; it becomes an identity that bleeds into how you work, express frustration, and even how you love.

That drive to outperform—to win—can push men into rougher, more physical forms of expression. It's part of what makes us more likely to respond to pressure with conflict, to get into fights, to lash out, or to carry anger in our bodies that we were never taught to talk about.

Men, however, are not the only ones who reinforce this model. Women are often socialized to desire the same traits society rewards in men. Many women are attracted to strength, height, and dominance because, historically, those traits were tied to protection and survival.

The first time competition took on a real personal significance was when I took the *StrengthsFinder 2.0* assessment from Tom Rath's book of the same name. The StrengthsFinder assessment is a tool developed by Gallup to help individuals discover their natural strengths. Competition showed up in my top five, along with ideation, innovation, strategic, and command. These results weren't a surprise, but seeing them on paper gave me language to use. It made something I had always felt instinctively more tangible in an instant.

According to StrengthFinders 2.0, people with the competition theme are driven by a desire to compare themselves to others and strive for excellence. They strive to win first place and revel in contests. They are intuitively aware of how others are performing and find themselves working hard to excel. Competition is rooted in comparison.

The more I've reflected, the more I've realized that a life lived in constant comparison can be exhausting. When your compass is always pointing toward better than, it becomes harder to ask yourself what matters. Especially when you're not really sure why you're in conflict, when you're following a script that tells you to maximize performance at all costs, often without questioning why or for whom we're doing it.

It reminds me of a story in the Bible called the parable of the talents.

The Parable of the Talents

The story goes like this:

A master is going away on a long journey. Before he leaves, he calls in three of his servants and gives each of them a portion of his wealth to manage. One gets five talents, another two, and the last servant only got one. The master doesn't give the servants any specific instructions on what to do with the talents, emphasizing stewardship.

"Do something with this. I trust you."

The first two take what they've been given and multiply it. The one with five turns those talents into ten. The one with two turns them into four. When the master returns, he praises them both.

"Well done. You were faithful with a little. Now I'll trust you with more."

But the third servant, who received only one talent, buried it in the ground. When the master asked why, he said, "I was afraid." He was afraid to fail, afraid of doing it wrong.

He buried his potential, so the master cast him out. Like the servant, many of us bury what we were meant to grow. Our fear leads us to live smaller, safer lives than we were designed for.

Now, depending on how you were raised, that story might have felt like fuel or proof that you have to hustle. You have to show results or risk being cast out.

Because I was successful in school and showed early promise, my parents pushed me to excel. I grew up knowing how to work hard and never gave in to mediocre performance or results. That mindset helped me cultivate discipline and it gave me drive. It helped me multiply what I was given, like the first two servants.

But here's what my parents, while giving me that push, didn't teach me: how to process fear. How to sit with uncertainty without immediately translating it into action. This is where the parable also becomes a warning. The third servant's fear overrode his actions. And yet in high-performing environments, we often do the opposite: We override our feelings to keep performing. We bury discomfort and trade inner clarity for outer results. There has to be balance both ways for us to truly succeed.

My takeaway from this lesson isn't only "don't waste your talent." It's this: *Using your gifts is essential, but not at the cost of your inner world.* It wasn't that the third servant's failure disappointed the master; it was that the third servant didn't even try because he was frozen in fear. We need to be able to decide how to act from a place of dealing with our fears instead of ignoring them—even if that means we need to take a break to adjust our mindset. Real stewardship means tending to both what you can do and how you feel while doing it. If you sacrifice one for the other, your success will always feel incomplete. And since we're discussing success, let's talk about what it really looks like for men in our present world.

Inherited Definitions of Success

Most men today grew up in systems that taught us to strive, perform, and suppress. Somewhere along the way, we learned that being a man meant being a provider and being in control. We were praised for pushing through and discouraged from slowing down. Vulnerability was seen as weakness, stillness was mistaken for laziness, and self-sacrifice was applauded, even when it meant physical, emotional, or relational self-neglect.

We started building our lives based on what we were told mattered: status, salary, and structure. Even when those things represented loving acts, such as working hard to support aging parents or giving our kids more opportunities than we had, we didn't stop to ask if the way we were doing things was sustainable, or if those choices actually fulfilled us.

In the same way that the servant in the parable buried his talent out of fear, many of us have followed narrow models of success out of fear of failure or disapproval. We've become one-dimensional in our definitions, prioritizing productivity and performance while neglecting presence and peace.

So, what creates a fulfilled life? It's certainly not status and salary on their own. You may have the corner office, a calendar booked weeks out, and a salary that makes life look easy from the outside. But on the inside, if you can't remember the last time you felt unrushed, unguarded, or truly at peace, do you really feel gratified?

Over the years, my core goals have not changed. I still want the same things I've always wanted. It's my understanding of how to pursue these goals and what matters in the process that has shifted significantly.

Incorporating the three pillars—self, home, and work—into the definition of success often requires a reprioritization, not of the destination, but of the way we go about getting there. It's a reexamination of how our goals are distributed and how much attention and energy we're devoting to each part of our lives.

Take a moment to consider the things you want to achieve in life. How well do those goals fit into each of these buckets? How much development, how much "muscle," does each pillar need in order to support the life you're trying to build?

If all your ambitions live in one domain, for example at work, you haven't clearly defined goals for your family or personal milestones for your own growth and well-being, then it's fair to assume that one or more of your pillars is underdeveloped. And when that happens, it becomes nearly impossible to maintain balance among the three. We'll get more into the three pillars and balance in chapters 5 and 6, but for now it's important to know that this is why we can't afford to evaluate success on autopilot. We need to assess where we are, honestly and holistically.

Success Starts With Assessment

In order to find balance in all areas of life, we must start with a self-assessment.

The self-assessment begins with determining your definition of success. In traditional terms, most of us were raised with one definition: Success is independence. It's being a provider and not needing to rely on other people. It's about self-sufficiency, emotional control, and handling things yourself.

In this view your needs like connection, support, and emotional expression don't fit the script. We don't usually associate manhood with collaboration or empathy. We associate it with withstanding pressure. Be not the one who needs, but the one who provides.

We even associate "need" with poverty. The needy are the ones we're supposed to help, not the ones we're supposed to become. Needs are things we solve. We're supposed to have answers, not questions, especially not questions about ourselves.

Ironically this model of success may be the very thing keeping us from evolving, because it discourages self-inquiry. If we don't interrogate ourselves and ask honest questions, we can't build awareness. And without that awareness, we never confront the real gaps, the blind spots, the unspoken flaws, or the buried fears.

It's easy to celebrate the things we're good at. But growth comes when we're willing to address the areas where we need help. That's why introspection is essential to success.

To help you engage in self-assessment, take a moment to reflect on the following questions:

- Is the life you're currently living one you created by design, or are you performing a role someone else handed to you?

- Which part of you is being sacrificed to keep everything else running?

- Do you have goals in all three areas of your life (self, home, and work) or only one?

- If your success were judged by your weakest area—not your strongest—how would you be doing?

- How do you want to be remembered, and by whom?

When you've focused on only one area of your life, it's easy to let the other pillars slip through the cracks. It becomes a habit to prioritize one area over another, so much so that you may not even do it consciously. You're always on but never fully present. Your health and habits slide. You miss milestones that matter. You start to break down, internally or externally. You drift toward what's easiest, not what you truly need.

The first step to changing these habits is self-awareness. Once you see where your attention and action flow, you can realign and adjust until your energy is balanced.

Coming back to the image of condensation on a cold can: When the inner and outer climates meet—when who you are inside matches how you show up in the world—you become someone new. You're no longer someone who might burst when the difference in temperature becomes too extreme.

When you experience relief from the internal pressure, that inner shift ripples outward, allowing you to build more authentic relationships. Leadership, which was once about control or performance becomes a reflection of emotional congruence. That means leading in a way that aligns with your internal values and feelings, so that who you are on the inside matches how you show up on the outside. It's about showing up as your true self rather than acting out a role or performing for approval. From that grounded place your purpose becomes clearer, as does your peace and drive.

You become someone with a broader impact who makes a difference not only in your career, but in your family and community. You reconnect with your humanity, integrating emotional awareness, presence, and softness into your strength. And you develop greater internal peace by aligning your actions with your values and intentionally while nurturing your inner world as well as your success.

Ultimately, you find balance. And balance creates sustainability. That means you no longer have to overextend, overcompensate, or overperform in one area while silently losing ground in the others. Balance means all three pillars are supporting the same life, not competing.

But even with balance, life has a way of testing us. There are still challenges—some obvious, some hidden—that can erode that hard-earned equilibrium. Before we can fully embrace wholeness, we need to confront the core problems that stand between us and the life we want.

Chapter 4

The Three Problems That Stand Between You and Wholeness

To be yourself in a world that is constantly trying to make you something else is the greatest accomplishment.
–RALPH WALDO EMERSON

Regrets of the Dying

In 2009, a blog titled *Regrets of the Dying* went viral, later inspiring a bestselling book that broke down the top five regrets people have at the end of their lives.

The author, Bronnie Ware, spent many years as a palliative care worker, someone who aims to minimize suffering and maximize quality of life for patients with severe and frequently terminal illnesses. For most of her patients, Ware was by their side during the final months of their lives, offering both physical comfort and emotional presence as they prepared to say goodbye.

In her reflections, Ware noted that facing mortality often sparked profound personal growth in her patients, who moved through a range of emotions before ultimately finding peace. In that process, her patients consistently shared similar regrets when asked what they would have done differently. Their regrets included wishing they had:

- built up the courage to live a life true to themselves, not one led by other people's expectations;
- created confidence within themselves to express their feelings;
- allowed themselves more moments of happiness;
- stayed in touch with their friends better; and
- not invested so much time and effort into work throughout life.

Not too long after I read Ware's book, I saw a clip of the investor and philanthropist Charlie Munger talking about how he always wanted to go tuna fishing and he never did. At the time of filming, Munger was at the end of his life. It was too late for him to try to rectify that dream because the strength required to reel in the fish would have been too much for him.

In the clip, he reconciled his regret by commenting that sometimes you have to give things up. And while his words made it seem as if he were okay with missing out on the experience, it was clear that Munger wished that one aspect of his life had been different.

Munger died in 2023 at the age of 99, one month shy of his 100th birthday. He had been the vice chairman of Berkshire

Hathaway, Warren Buffet's investment company, since 1978. At the time of his death, his estimated net worth was $2.6 billion, according to Forbes.[4] If there was anyone who had the resources to go tuna fishing, it was Munger.

Munger didn't explain in the clip why he never went to catch tuna, and his regret could fall into several of Ware's categories. The category that seems to line up with this regret is most likely that he wished he'd allowed himself more happiness.

In Munger's story, we see that there's something healthy about being able to release old dreams when the time for them has passed, to accept that we won't cross off every item, we won't achieve it all, and that's simply part of being human. But there's this sadness to it too. In the 80 years of his adult life, Munger never prioritized this particular dream enough to make it happen. He died with the regret of not having that experience.

Regret, in the end, is rarely about failure. Instead it's about misalignment between who we are and how we're living. It's about having a poor configuration between what we say matters and where our time actually goes. It's a misalignment in the priority of the three pillars of our lives and the weight we place on each of them. At work, that regret might look like spending too much time chasing promotions and not enough time building something you're truly passionate about. At home, it might be missing too many family moments you won't be able to get back. When it comes to the self, it might be living a life that follows expectations but doesn't feel authentic to you.

---

4   "Charles Munger," *Forbes*, accessed April 17, 2025, https://www.forbes.com/profile/charles-munger/.

Ware's five regrets don't arise from laziness or lack of ambition. They each stem from trying to earn approval, avoid judgment, or meet expectations that don't always reflect who we are as individuals. Regrets like these emerge when we're too afraid to define success on our own terms.

At the root of these regrets are fears that quietly shape our choices, narrowing our lives until we're left wondering what could have been. But we don't have to wait until the end of our lives to see them clearly. We can name them now.

What follows are three core problems I've seen time and again in my own journey and in the lives of the men I've walked alongside. These are real, persistent patterns that keep us from experiencing the kind of presence, peace, and purpose we want. And unlike regret, these are patterns we still have time to change. Each problem maps directly to the regrets we explored earlier—they're the root causes behind the disconnection, unspoken feelings, missed joy, and misplaced priorities so many men carry. As we go through each problem, I'll show you where the different patterns emerge.

Problem #1: We Trade Wholeness for Performance

As we've already touched on, traditional masculinity conditions men to lead without emotion and to prioritize performance over well-being. Here, we'll dig deeper into how that conditioning creates patterns of emotional suppression, isolation, and burnout.

What we call personal behavior is often inherited belief. Before we ever chose how to show up, we were shaped by forces we couldn't name—culture, tradition, and expectation.

This conditioning is both a personal obstacle and a structural one. It was built before us and then passed down to us through generations, workplaces, media, and culture. Traditional masculinity has distorted the definition of strength, conditioning men in ways that distance them from themselves by promoting unhealthy concepts. Let's consider how these may impact our well-being.

Emotional Suppression: Traditional masculinity often promotes the idea that men should be stoic and emotionally hardened, leading them to suppress their feelings. This expectation discourages men from expressing vulnerability or seeking emotional support, which often results in a disconnect from their own emotions that hinders their ability to connect with others.

Prioritizing Work Over Self-Care: The societal expectation for men to be providers creates a strong emphasis on work and success. This pressure can lead men to prioritize their careers over their mental and emotional well-being. They may feel compelled to work long hours and sacrifice personal time, neglecting self-care and the nurturing of their relationships. This relentless focus on career achievements leads men to burn the candle at both ends, catalysing burnout and overall dissatisfaction in their lives.

Avoiding Help-Seeking Behaviors: The traditional view of masculinity often emphasizes self-reliance and independence, making it difficult for men to ask for help or support. This reluctance to seek assistance can prevent men from addressing their challenges effectively, whether in personal or professional contexts. It fosters a culture where men feel they must handle everything on their own, which can exacerbate feelings of isolation and stress.

These conditioning factors contribute to a cycle of emotional disconnection and unhealthy coping mechanisms, ultimately impacting men's mental health and relationships. When men are taught to hide what they feel, they struggle to express themselves clearly or to respond with empathy or to be fully present with the people they care about. Over time this erodes trust, weakens emotional bonds, and creates distance in the very relationships they value most.

When we follow these conditioned scripts long enough, we start sacrificing essential parts of ourselves to meet external demands. It creates a process I call self-cannibalism.

Cannibalizing Ourselves in the Name of Success

Men tend to cannibalize certain aspects of themselves for the sake of other priorities. For example, someone may throw themselves into work thinking that they are providing a better life for their child. They work 80 hours per week in order to pay for a life they never had the opportunity to experience as a kid, they buy their child expensive gifts, and provide for their children's every financial need. But by virtue of spending 80 hours a week at work, they're not giving their child time or attention.

That's an extreme example, but we see this all the time in less extreme ways. There's the father who is technically present, he shows up to the baseball games and the dance recitals, but he's constantly on his phone answering emails. Or the single executive who, after a long day at work, doom scrolls on social media or flips through the Netflix menu every night, watching shows or movies while eating junk food.

Many high-functioning men are cannibalizing themselves in the name of success without realizing it. When one of the three pillars is starved and another overfed, the system turns on itself.

You might be thriving at work, checking off milestones and earning accolades, but you're missing critical moments at home. You're pushing your body past its limits. You're emotionally unavailable. And instead of recognizing this as unsustainable, you double down, convincing yourself that you have to push through and accept the conditioning I've mentioned in this section because that's what you've been taught strength looks like.

We exist as whole people. You are a whole person. I am a whole person. When evaluating your life, you have to take your entire life into consideration and recognize that you can't be everywhere all at once. You can't be something to others that you aren't first to yourself.

When we overextend in one space, we're consuming our internal reserves. That fatigue shows up in our patience, our presence, and our peace. You need to put your oxygen mask on first. You can't be generous and giving to others, without resentment and in a sustainable way, if you haven't first taken care of yourself—the pillar of self

And it works the other way, too. When you cannibalize your home pillar to fuel your work pillar, you may hit your goals, but the cost is missed memories and relationships that run on autopilot. The opposite is also true: When you cannibalize work to overcompensate at home—saying yes to everything, carrying more than your share, trying to "make up for" past absences—you may start falling behind professionally.

We exist physically in all three spaces. We play critical roles in each space as fathers, husbands, leaders, and human beings. We pull from one part of our lives to sustain another, and eventually, that depletion catches up with us.

Think about nourishment in the body. When we eat a balanced diet, our bodies take what they need and store the rest for later. But when we stop giving the body the fuel it needs, whether from neglect, stress, or intentional restriction, it shuts down and literally starts to break itself down to survive. It consumes muscle as it begins to feed on itself.

When we're out of balance, we start pulling energy, time, and emotional presence from wherever we can find it. We pull from the self pillar if we're not getting enough rest; from the home pillar, if connection and intimacy have been deprioritized; or from the work pillar, when burnout steals our focus and clarity.

Biologically this process of trying to find equilibrium under pressure is called homeostasis. The body is full of systems designed to maintain balance: temperature, circulation, and respiration. They're constantly working behind the scenes to keep things steady, even when conditions aren't ideal. But when we push those systems too far without support, they fail.

It's the same in our lives. If we neglect to nourish each pillar with intention, attention, and care, we risk the same kind of imbalance. One area becomes overfed and bloated with responsibility, while another goes hungry. We diminish our strength to keep up the appearance of stability. But no system, not even the body, can survive on self-consumption forever. That internal depletion affects our emotional availability. And when vulnerability feels unsafe or unfamiliar, many of us default to hiding what we feel instead of facing it.

Problem #2: We Value Emotional Suppression

Traditional masculinity has conditioned men to suppress their emotions by promoting the idea that expressing feelings or showing vulnerability of any kind is a sign of weakness. As a result, men have been robbed of their full humanity, discouraged from expressing emotions that are intrinsic to the human experience.

Men are often socialized to view fear as a weakness, leading them to suppress feelings of anxiety. Expressing sadness is frequently seen as a sign of emotional fragility, which can be stigmatized in masculine cultures. Feelings of insecurity or self-doubt are typically viewed as unmanly, causing men to hide these emotions rather than confront them. Even expressing positive emotions like joy, happiness, or compassion can be perceived as overly emotional or not serious enough, especially in certain professional or social contexts.

The act of being vulnerable, whether through sharing personal struggles or seeking help, is often discouraged, as it contradicts the ideal of self-sufficiency. Men are taught to be stoic and to handle challenges independently, which discourages them from seeking help or sharing their struggles. Because of this, many men are afraid to open up and reveal authentic emotional expressions worrying how others will perceive them.

This conditioning leads to a focus on work and external achievements over self-care and emotional well-being, as men feel pressured to fulfill the role of provider and to demonstrate strength. In a way, we hide parts of ourselves and create a facade of invulnerability rather than show up in the world as we truly are. As a result, men often neglect their own needs and the importance of emotional connection, ultimately leading to an unbalanced life where personal fulfillment and relationships suffer. When we don't know how to express what we feel, we not only lose touch with ourselves, we also miss the chance to be truly seen by others.

Excluding certain emotions from the definition of masculinity has created a one-dimensional view of what it means to be a man. We've been too narrow in our thinking around what leadership is and what it can look like. As I mentioned early on, these patterns don't make us stronger, they make us brittle.

Confronting the parts of ourselves we've been taught to see as weaknesses is actually what makes us stronger. It's what gives us depth, resilience, and emotional elasticity. When we stop avoiding discomfort and start integrating our full emotional range, we become more well-rounded and more relatable.

On the other hand, if we hold on to the narrow definition we've been given, and we foster the inability to express vulnerability or seek help, this can create barriers in our personal connections. Over time, this leads to loneliness and disconnection. This was pointed out to me on a personal level while I attended a program at Harvard Business School. Allow me to explain.

The Challenge of Genuine Connection

During the program, I had a one-on-one call with a professor who asked what I wanted to improve. I told her: connecting with people. She smiled and said my answer made her like me a whole lot more.

At first I wasn't sure how to take that. Was she saying she hadn't liked me before? It's possible. I'd been showing up in that space much like I've shown up in many others: focused, intellectual, and driven. I was there for the cases, the debates, and the high-level conversations. Those are the things that I find exhilarating. I love a good debate where you can really dig into a topic. But not everyone is wired that way. Not everyone wants to go as deep as I might want to or connect through intensity or shared analysis.

One of my professors told me that I'm hard to read. It's something I've heard many times before, and I can see why people think that. I can be stoic. I like to observe and process, and I don't always clue people in to what I'm thinking or feeling. It's not that I'm intentionally distancing myself from others; these actions come from a habit of self-containment. This is an emotional armor I've worn for most of my life. But as I had this discussion with my professor, I realized the armor I felt made me look strong also prevented others from connecting with me. It acted as an effective barrier between myself and others, as I had built it to function.

My professor offered me some advice. She told me to open up to new groups of people and address it up front that I'm not the type of guy who is great at making small talk. That's an extremely vulnerable admission to make, especially to strangers I'm meeting for the first time. However, by setting the expectation through vulnerability, I was better able to overcome that initial barrier and create deeper connections.

For many men, forming bonds is a challenge. But connection is essential to the human experience. It's a part of Maslow's hierarchy of needs—a psychological theory proposed by Abraham Maslow that outlines five levels of human needs that individuals strive to fulfill. The desire to connect is there, underneath all the bravado and denial. The challenge around building effective relationships comes from not being taught to access connections in meaningful ways.

A lot of connection is meaningless: It's proximity-based and superficial. Real connection that is deep and meaningful with another human being usually doesn't happen in a group. It happens one-on-one. That's when people are more likely to be vulnerable, to open up.

But how often do men actually sit down for one-on-one conversations? How often do we go beyond small talk, beyond sports and work updates, to talk about what we're afraid of, where we're struggling, and areas where we wish to improve?

There's a cultural bias at play here, an undercurrent that says emotional conversations are "feminine," that small groups and intimate dialogue are soft. And because we associate softness with weakness, we avoid the very settings that are most likely to create a genuine connection.

It's easier to brag than to talk about what we're bad at. It's easier to talk about trades or sports than problems in your marriage or frustrations at work. This discomfort doesn't mean we're incapable of making true connections. It means we have been under-trained in emotional awareness. We don't have the skills that help relationships work.

Connection isn't something you either have or you don't. It's promoted by a learned skill set. And many of those skills—empathy, listening, vulnerability, self-disclosure—get dismissed under the label of soft skills.

So part of making vulnerability feel safer comes from reframing this idea of soft skills into life skills. If you can better connect, better communicate, better listen, and be honest with yourself, you'll build stronger relationships with others and with yourself.

This reframe is critical. We've been taught to think of emotional openness as optional—as extra. But in truth, it's foundational. You can't lead if you can't connect. And you can't connect if you can't push past the discomfort of being vulnerable.

There is so much more to say about the importance of vulnerability. This is why, in chapter six, we'll dive deeper into reframing vulnerability as strength and explore how it can make you a better leader, friend, partner, and parent. But for now, let's take a look at the final problem that stands between you and wholeness.

Problem #3: We Reach for Control Instead of Facing the Root Issue

There's a pattern many of us fall into, especially those of us who identify as high-functioning men. When emotions rise, relationships strain, or restlessness creeps in, we don't stop to reflect. Instead, we double down. We reach for more work, more structure, more distraction—anything that gives us a stronger sense of control.

And at first glance, it looks like discipline, or hard work, or drive. But beneath the surface, something else is happening. We're reaching for the aspects of life that we can control rather than looking inward and facing the root of the problem.

For example, when I was studying for the CPA exam, it seemed like I was getting everything done except for studying. You've likely experienced this in your own life. When there is something important to do, suddenly the yard is mowed, the car has been washed, the fridge is full of groceries, and you've spontaneously found the time to check off every item on your to-do list except for the thing that really needed to get done.

There is a book called *Eat That Frog!* by Brian Tracy that outlines 21 tips to stop procrastination. His biggest tip? Tackle the hardest task first before moving on to easier ones. If we can consistently face the hard thing—that one thing we tend to avoid—that's when real change begins.

The hardest task is usually the thing we're least comfortable doing. It's the action we're afraid to take: the one that we procrastinate on the most. The item we keep pushing to the bottom of the list, even though we know it's exactly what needs our attention.

I find that in the context of finding balance in the three pillars of life, the hard thing men avoid most is facing the emotional, relational, and internal work.

Doing the internal work is essential because it's the only path toward wholeness, and in turn, sustainable leadership, emotional presence, and, most importantly, long-term fulfillment.

The internal work is about getting to the root of the uneasiness we feel, like when you're surrounded by your family at home but still feel distant and distracted. When you're constantly achieving at work but never feel a true sense of arrival. When your patience runs thin for no obvious reason, or when you're irritable with the people you love most and can't quite explain why. When you're up late scrolling, pouring another drink, or working through the weekend because you just don't know how to sit still or take care of self.

It's the work of asking not just *What am I doing?* but *Why am I doing it?*

We use avoidance as a band-aid to cover up the root of the problem because facing that root is hard. It requires honesty and effort. It takes time to delve into it, and it might require professional help or feedback from others, which requires vulnerability.

Real work is hard, which is why we like to ignore the problem and turn to the things we can more easily control. But when you struggle alone with your challenges instead of reaching out for assistance, that can lead you into isolation which reinforces a sense of inadequacy inside you. In contrast, control can *feel* like safety, but in relationships, control often becomes a wall between us and the people we care about most.

Sustainable change doesn't come from doing more. It comes from aligning what we do with what truly matters and having the courage to stay with what truly matters long enough to grow.

When Control Becomes Collapse

When emotional disconnection, loneliness, and unprocessed pain go unaddressed long enough, they often manifest in ways that are hard to recognize until it's too late: substance use, domestic violence, emotional shutdown, and even suicide.

According to the CDC, men in the US are nearly four times more likely to die by suicide than women.[5] They're also more likely to misuse alcohol and drugs[6] and less likely to seek mental health support.[7]

These patterns are rooted in culture. They reflect the cost of a system that teaches men to bottle up what hurts, to armor up in the face of pain, and to equate silence with strength. Violence,

---

5   Centers for Disease Control and Prevention, *Suicide Mortality in the United States*, 2021.

6   National Institute on Drug Abuse, *Substance Use in Men*, 2020.

7   American Psychological Association, *Men and Mental Health: Barriers to Treatment*. 2018.

addiction, and despair don't emerge from nowhere; they are often the aftershocks of a man collapsing under the weight of who he was told to be.

From an early age, men are socialized to suppress emotional pain and avoid asking for help. Stoicism is prized while vulnerability is punished. Expressing sadness or softness becomes taboo, while expressions of anger and dominance are rewarded. As a result, many men internalize the belief that discomfort must be managed privately—if at all—and that control is the only acceptable coping strategy to avoid the consequences of refusing to acknowledge and process their feelings.

But this type of control eventually collapses. What begins as withdrawal or overworking can quietly evolve into self-harm, substance dependency, or emotional implosion. When men are only taught to be strong, they're given no tools for what to do when they feel weak.

When we look at the statistics and see rising rates of male suicide, addiction, and violence, it's not due to the failure of individual men. It's the result of a flawed emotional blueprint. One that elevates independence over interdependence, aggression over attunement, and silence over self-awareness.

If we want to reclaim our wholeness, we have to stop looking away. We have to find the root, name the pain, and begin the deeper work of healing it.

Each of these problems doesn't just affect how we feel internally, they all shape how we show up in our relationships at work, at home, and in our communities. Until we address them, our ability to lead and connect will remain limited.

Living Without Regrets

The problems we've explored in this chapter—following outdated conditioning, hiding behind invulnerability, and reaching for control instead of facing what's real—are patterns. Patterns shaped by culture, passed down through generations, and reinforced by the systems we live in. When left unchecked, they lead to the very regrets we opened this chapter with: disconnection, unexpressed emotion, and missed opportunities for joy.

The good news is that patterns can be disrupted and replaced with something far more sustainable, human, and whole. What you've begun to do in this chapter is name the problem. And naming it is the first act of power.

From here, we will shift from recognizing the barriers to building the foundation for lasting change. In the next chapter, we'll explore the Three Pillars of the New Alpha and how aligning your energy across these three areas can help you reclaim your sense of purpose, presence, and peace.

Chapter 5

Servant Leadership Across the Three Pillars

*The first responsibility of a leader is to define reality. The
last is to say thank you. In between,
the leader is a servant.*
–Max De Pree

Servant Leadership

In this chapter, I want to explore how the principles of servant leadership apply not only to boardrooms or businesses, but to the way we show up in every corner of our lives. The heart of this book is about becoming a better leader through balance, not dominance. Servant leadership reflects this theme by challenging the definition of the kind of leadership that prizes control and constant output, replacing it with a model rooted in presence and emotional integrity.

At its core, servant leadership flips the traditional model of power. Instead of people existing to serve the leader, the leader exists to serve the people. Servant leadership prioritizes the growth, well-being, and development of others. It's a leadership model grounded in emotional intelligence and long-term stewardship.

The term was first coined by Robert K. Greenleaf in his 1970 essay "The Servant as Leader."[8] Greenleaf believed that the best leaders weren't those who sought authority for themselves; they began with a desire to serve.

There are ten core traits[9] that define a servant leader:

- Listening
- Empathy
- Healing
- Awareness
- Persuasion over coercion
- Conceptualization
- Foresight
- Stewardship
- Commitment to the growth of people
- Building Community

These traits are strategically necessary for leaders across every area of life, especially in today's world where trust, adaptability, and emotional intelligence are nonnegotiables in strong leadership.

This is the attitude we're applying across the three pillars.

---

8   Robert K. Greenleaf, "The Servant as Leader," (Indianapolis: The Robert K. Greenleaf Center, 1970).

9   Larry C. Spears, "Ten Characteristics of a Servant Leader," *The Spears Center for Servant-Leadership*, November 1, 2018, https://www.spearscenter.org/images/stories/Ten_Characteristics_of_a_Servant_Leader_by_Larry_Spears_11.01.18.pdf.

Applying Servant Leadership Across Pillars

So, how do we apply this kind of leadership across the full landscape of our lives?

In the old alpha model, we've been taught to measure our worth by what we produce. We define success by metrics like promotions, income, and status. But that kind of one-dimensional, outward facing success often comes at the cost of our inner well-being. Servant leadership invites us to look beyond these metrics and to reflect on how we interact with others and ourselves as well. Becoming a servant leader across the three pillars has us consider things like:

- How emotionally available we are at home
- Whether our actions align with our values
- How well we care for ourselves
- The depth of our relationships
- The integrity we have across all areas of our lives

The three pillars offer a framework for practicing this broader standard, one that goes beyond measuring success at work. Let's take a closer look at each pillar and how we can apply servant leadership to each.

Servant Leadership to the Self

I want to start with the self pillar because this is the area of life that is most often neglected and yet the most fundamental to all relationships. When we have a good understanding of ourselves and a balance of discipline and compassion within the self pillar, we create a fertile space for relationships to flourish. But if the self is out of balance, we become like a seed in acidic soil under insufficient light: very little will take root and grow.

We've been taught to polish the outside and ignore the inside. We'll spend hours washing our cars, grooming our hair, or dressing in our best clothes. And when it comes to our inner world—our thoughts, emotions, and spiritual health—we often look the other way. It's like driving around in a car that is kept in immaculate condition with a filthy, junk-filled house that has piles hidden behind closed doors. We're taught that our worth is tied to our accomplishments, our appearance, and our performance; we're encouraged to ignore our mental and emotional health.

The self is also the only pillar that doesn't come with an outward scoreboard. At work, metrics and promotions guide and validate us. At home, kids and partners create their own forms of measurement, feedback, and accountability. There are no immediate consequences for skipping reflection, rest, or emotional check-ins. We can avoid our inner selves for years and still appear to the outer world as a high-functioning adult. We can be praised, promoted, even admired, while continuing to be hollow men.

Culturally, we've been taught that focusing on ourselves is selfish. Rest is often equated with laziness, or at minimum a lack of progress. Emotional needs are considered optional or indulgent. Ironically, many of us account for this by indulging in other ways to compensate, in the same way that when we are tired, we tend to eat and drink more. We've been taught to suppress our needs and overwork as another form of distraction. We stay busy to distract ourselves from the deeper questions about our purpose, emotions, needs, and the gaps between who we are and who we want to be.

We also cannot lead others if we've lost ourselves. This is one of many reasons all of us need to embrace servant leadership.

Applying Servant Leadership to the Self

Servant leadership isn't only a management style, it's a way of being that can deeply influence relationships in all areas of life, including your relationship with yourself. In fact, stable leadership requires a healthy and calm relationship with oneself. Because the self is often the most neglected pillar, falling short here lowers the strength of every other pillar.

Servant leadership in relation to the self is about serving the *future you* while being kind to the *present you*.

This can show up as practicing self-compassion instead of harsh inner criticism. It can also mean taking care of your mental and physical health so you can sustain your service to others. It may be doing something as simple as engaging in reflection, like asking: *Am I living in a way that aligns with my values?*

Servant leadership is about being the kind of leader to yourself that you would want to be for others. That means creating boundaries that protect your well-being as well as your productivity. It means noticing your patterns, reflecting on your values, and staying accountable to the life you say you want.

To use an example from my own life, during the COVID-19 pandemic, I began to think deeply about how I was actually spending my time, and what I'd do with that time if I didn't have to work. I wanted to make sure that every moment reflected what really mattered to *me*. That's when I took a closer look at my personal finance journey through the lens of the FIRE movement, which stands for Financial Independence, Retire Early. I realized that financial freedom wasn't only about money; it was about creating space to do the things that make me feel alive—whether that's traveling, writing, or giving back.

FIRE contests the idea that you need to work until the end of life by stating that people don't find gratification from work alone. In addition to your career, you may want to learn new skills, spend more time with family, or move to the countryside and start a farm. The point of FIRE is to define your values and let those values guide your financial and personal choices. Like applying servant leadership to the self, FIRE encourages you to intentionally live in a way that aligns with your values.

Most of us are on a path we started as teenagers, often based on someone else's idea of what we should do with our lives or undeveloped and untested notions of our own imaginations. So to lead yourself well, it's important to consider what brings you peace, fulfillment, and a true sense of accomplishment. For most people, professional careers alone will not be enough to achieve the type of "self actualization" that Maslow describes— that highest level of human motivation, where we strive to reach our full potential and become the most authentic, developed, and enlightened versions of ourselves. At that level, we don't only grow for ourselves; we become a beacon of light, illuminating the path for others to follow and inspiring them to reach for their highest potential too. Strong leadership begins with first serving ourselves well.

Isolating in the pandemic offered me the opportunity to reflect on all this and to consider whether I was living up to my potential and making the greatest contributions I could, while still doing things that made me happy. As I reflected on the kind of legacy I wanted to leave behind, I was reminded that it wasn't all about personal success, and that personal success is often too narrowly defined. My definition of success was about being a good partner, a good father to my daughter, a good son to my parents, and finding ways to give back to my various communities while inspiring others to do the same. That reflection led me to establish a scholarship in my family's name at the University of the Bahamas, which I attended, and to stay committed to doing philanthropic work that can truly change lives.

I also began the *Executive Dad* podcast to share this message with others and to initiate the kinds of conversations that have been missing for too long. While doing the podcast, ideas began to crystalize and the core ideas of what this book aims to resolve began building in my mind. Through these pages, I want to continue constructing that vision of emotionally enriched, self-aware men who communicate effectively. You can be all this and more, becoming even stronger while learning how to be a better leader in the process.

All of that—slowing down, reevaluating, realigning—was my way of practicing servant leadership toward myself. It meant honoring not only the man I was, but the man I was becoming. It meant creating space to grow without burning out and to contribute without abandoning my true self. That's what servant leadership to the self is at its core: leading yourself with the same care, clarity, and commitment you'd offer anyone you're responsible for. Now let's look at servant leadership inside the next pillar: home.

Servant Leadership in the Home

Many men walk into their homes carrying the same mindset they've been rewarded for at work: be the provider, be in control, and be the man who gets things done. They see themselves as the authority, the anchor, the one people depend on, and certainly the one to whom people should listen. But what they don't realize is that being the provider, or even the "top dog," doesn't make you a participant in your family.

As men we often define our roles as fathers through sacrifice. We think being gone all day, working long hours, giving our children what *we* didn't have growing up is the full, or at least primary, measure of love.

This approach creates habits where men come home, act in a dominant way—as a leader in the home dynamic—but still not really present. Perhaps this is the worst combination because you are physically there and everyone knows it, but you're not mentally or emotionally there and your absence is felt by your family. Small but important needs from your partner or child get trivialized or ignored. Everyone struggles with the distance they feel even when together, maybe especially then. That confusion, that ache, stems from a lack of meaningful and productive engagement. And without you making an effort to rethink what it really means to lead at home, that gap between you and the people you love most will only grow.

This disconnection erodes communication, trust, and emotional relatability. You might still be doing the school drop-offs, paying the mortgage, and showing up for dinner, but under the surface, the relationship is fraying. Conversations become shallow. Affection feels forced or routine. Maybe conversation and attraction disappear altogether or are even replaced with smoldering hostilities and tension. You're doing what you think your family *needs* instead of asking them what they actually *want*, and they get frustrated and set in their own perspectives. Your intentions are good, but perhaps your unilateral vision and the accompanying execution are not. So how will you address this as a balanced leader, rather than a dominant one?

Applying Servant Leadership at Home

Ask yourself and your family: Does our home feel like a community? There's a difference between being in the same house and being in the same rhythm. The truth is, you can be physically present but emotionally out of sync. Rhythm means you're aware of what's happening in your household, not just the schedule, but the energy, the mood, and the emotional needs.

One reason many men struggle to build that rhythm is because home doesn't operate like work. You might be doing what's required, but without knowing the rhythm, you're managing a household, not leading your small and vital community.

A big trap that many men fall into is compartmentalization. We tell ourselves that we can separate who we are at work from who we are at home, and who we are privately from both. But we're not three different people. We're one person living in three different contexts. And whether we want to admit it or not, those contexts bleed into one another.

When you're emotionally depleted from overextending at work, that fatigue doesn't stay in the office. It shows up in your tone with your kids, in the way you disengage at the dinner table, or in how unavailable you become to your partner. The same nervous system goes to work, goes home, and goes to sleep at night. If your nervous system is overstimulated or undernourished in one area, it doesn't flip a switch when you walk through a different door.

When we compartmentalize, we lose sight of how our actions feel to the people around us. We may think we're protecting our loved ones by keeping stress from work out of the house, or that disappearing into overwork is a noble way to provide. But from the outside, that absence feels like neglect.

That's why we have to examine the stories we've been telling ourselves about sacrifice. We assume that as long as we're working hard and providing materially, we're doing the right thing. Often we're offering what looks like love from a distance and focusing mainly on money, while withholding the very things that build intimacy: time, attention, and support.

You can be doing all the right things and still be missing the mark if your family never actually gets to experience you. That's why the leadership you practice at home has to be relational, not hierarchical. Even if you're leading in the home, you also need to be by your family's side, supporting them, and undergirding their efforts.

In this book, we're reframing this perception that leadership means domination. We're creating the new mindset that leadership is about helping others to achieve an objective and ensuring that your team has buy-in and support. This form of leadership applies as much to a family dinner table as it does to a team meeting. True servant leadership in the home means making space for others to speak, grow, and contribute.

Servant leadership in family life centers around kind acts, emotional presence, and supportive empowerment. This may look like listening deeply to partners and children without immediately offering solutions.

Servant leadership in the home prioritizes the growth and well-being of family members. For example, supporting a partner's career dreams or a child's interests. It looks like modeling patience, empathy, and humility—especially during conflicts—and sharing responsibilities rather than asserting control or appealing to hierarchy.

A servant-leader parent asks their child, "How can I support you right now?" instead of saying, "Here's what you need to do."

The goal is not to be the hero. You're there to help build the environment in a collaborative way with others, not to dictate what it should look like. Open collaboration builds trust and respect. And over time, it builds a kind of leadership that lasts longer than any rule or routine ever could.

Finally, let's look at how this type of leadership functions in the professional world.

Servant Leadership at Work

For many men, work is more than a career; it's a part of their identity. It's where we feel competent, respected, and in control. It's where we get the accolades, feel satisfied or a sense of authority and respect. So, naturally, this is the pillar that tends to get the most attention.

We often treat overworking like it's a solution. We tell ourselves we're doing it for the family, for the future, for stability. But more often than not, we're filling our calendars because movement feels like progress. We get busy doing everything else so we don't have to face what's really there—the unresolved conflict with a partner, the burnout none of us want to admit, the version of success that no longer fits. Instead of pausing, we double down. We grind harder. We justify our absence with productivity. And in doing so, we turn work into the most socially acceptable form of escape.

What makes prioritizing the pillar of work so tricky is that it looks responsible from the outside. No one questions a man who's putting in the hours, climbing the ladder, or staying late for the team. But behind that performance, many of us use work as a place to avoid the problems we have in other pillars. We convince ourselves that if we keep going, we won't have to feel whatever it is we don't want to feel. What we don't face eventually follows us into our homes, our health, and our relationships that matter most.

Your team at work might respect you, but they won't raise your children. They won't sit with you in the hospital. They won't hold your hand when you're old. The people who will, your family and your inner circle, are often the ones most impacted by your absence.

At some point, I had to ask myself, *Why am I really doing all this?* It's easy to say you're doing it for your family or for stability or for the legacy you want to leave behind. Is that true? Or are you replaying someone else's definition of success?

I realized that a lot of what I was striving for came from a place of lack. We tend to define success based on what we didn't have growing up. Because I didn't have something back then doesn't mean that thing is what my family actually needs from me today. They don't need the version of success I used to daydream about as a kid. They need me. Whole, healthy, and present. That means asking not only what or who I'm working for, but who I'm becoming through my work.

Applying Servant Leadership at Work

Once I started getting honest about why I work, and who I'm really doing it for, I realized my approach to leadership had to change.

For a long time I thought being a good leader meant being the smartest one in the room with the answers and the one who drives results. But that version of leadership is often more about protecting your own status than it is about developing the people around you.

Servant leadership flips that. It encourages us to ask, *How am I creating space for others to grow? Am I leading through people, or over them? Am I making room for their voices, their visions, and their value as human beings, or am I trying to move them toward my voice, vision, and value?*

Servant leadership at work means I don't only care about the outcome; I also care about how we get there. I care about who grows in the process and whether the people I lead feel seen, heard, and empowered.

Leadership is about thinking strategically. But it's also about observing other people's experiences so you can reflect on how to serve them better. It's about trying to make as big an impact as possible on others so that you can create as much fulfillment for them as possible.

This may look like leaders putting the needs of the team above personal ambition or ego. It's mentoring and coaching employees toward their goals. It could be leaders making decisions that benefit the collective, not just shareholders or senior leaders, or acknowledging the contributions of others and celebrating their wins.

As a servant leader, you lead by lifting others, not by controlling them. In the workplace, servant leadership fosters collaboration and trust—and emphasizes the development of others.

Finding Balance Between and Within Each Pillar

Servant leadership across the three pillars means showing up with the same integrity and emotional presence in every role you occupy. While often thought of as separate categories, each pillar is interrelated and a disruption in one area can impact the others. Therefore, it is crucial to pay attention to all three pillars to maintain balance.

It's also essential to note the need for balance *within* each pillar, not just between them. We've talked about how neglecting one area can disrupt another. Challenges can also arise inside a single pillar.

When I say it's important to find balance, I don't mean that you will find an equal balance between each pillar at all times. As we'll discuss in the next chapter, balance is dynamic and fluid. We're often teetering between these categories based on individual circumstances and needs at any given time.

Part 2

Reconnection

Chapter 6

The Art of Wobbling Well

Life is like riding a bicycle. To keep your balance,
you must keep moving.
–ALBERT EINSTEIN

How Balance Really Works

You may think of balance and imagine perfect stillness, two sides equally stabilized on a scale. In reality, it's not a frozen moment because our lives don't stop. Balance is momentum. It's forward motion in spite of the possibility for things to topple over.

Think about riding a bicycle. When you first learn, every muscle in your body tenses, fighting to keep you upright. You're wobbly on those two wheels as you constantly overcorrect, moving from side to side. You might panic and slam your feet on the ground because stillness feels safer than falling.

There lies the fundamental flaw: On a bike, standing still is exactly when you're most likely to fall. You have to embrace the movement; it's the forward movement—the messy pedaling, the shifting of weight, the tiny adjustments—that keeps you up.

Pedaling relies on imbalance: pressure on the left pedal, then the right, then the left again. Constant switching creates the movement that holds the balance.

If you ever watch professional bicycle riders sprinting toward the finish line, you will see an incredible amount of wobbling under the power of that momentum. You will not often see the riders fall. You'll see an overall sense of balance with the wobbling as a part of the broader process.

If a rider does tumble, they don't stay down. They get back up, mount their bike, and drive that imperfect momentum forward again. It's their commitment to keep pedaling, to keep moving forward, that restores their balance.

What is balance then if it isn't the *absence* of wobble? Balance is the skill of *wobbling well*. The same is true not only on a bicycle, but in our daily lives.

We've been taught to chase a perfect, fixed idea of balance. For many of us, this looks like a neatly divided schedule. Take the 24 hours in a day and divide it evenly into three sections: eight hours for work, eight for leisure, and eight for sleep. This division is fine in theory, but this kind of symmetry doesn't exist in our daily lives. At least not in a sustainable way.

In life, as on a bike, standing still leads to falling over. It's the willingness to keep moving—to wobble, to adjust, to lean a little too far, and then shift back—that keeps us upright. But it goes beyond that. Since you are a partner and a father, you have to help your family find balance. It is often a father's responsibility to teach his children how to ride a bike.

Your Imbalance Affects Others

Balance, like life, isn't something we manage in isolation. Every shift we make, every moment of overcorrection, hesitation, or acceleration sends ripples outward, touching the people moving alongside us. Our imbalance doesn't stay contained. The actions we take affect the lives of everyone around us.

Think about those professional cyclists again. Not only do riders sometimes fall on their own, they often collide or hit and fall over one another. Balance isn't a solo act. Each rider moves independently, yet must maintain balance as part of something larger than themselves.

We're not solitary planets spinning safely on our own. We're part of a larger system, constantly moving in and out of each other's orbit as we navigate our path. The same is true in life. Our families, coworkers, and friends are all balancing their own shifting paths as they continue forward. When we move, when we stumble, when we surge ahead or fall behind, it naturally affects the stability of those around us. To find momentum, we must understand that we wobble together with those around us. Our wobble can change the emotional environment in a room, a home, or a team. Without even meaning to, our internal imbalance can destabilize those we care about most. When we are intentional, our efforts to regain balance can inspire and steady those same people too.

When you collide or cut off one another at work or at home, that is when you need to know how to disentangle and reengage. Do you sit there squabbling, complaining, and licking your wounds? Do you hold out your limbs so that others can see how you've been wounded?

Hopefully not, since those would be pointless endeavors in the long run. It may be a part of your overall rebalancing process, and yet you don't want to stay static or out of balance for too long. Recovery, after all, depends not only on regaining your footing; it depends on understanding what balance looks like for *you*, specifically, in the first place.

There is no single way to move or act to achieve balance. What balance is for me isn't what balance is for you. Balance is deeply personal, shaped by the unique pressures, priorities, and challenges that each one of us carries. Though balance must be defined on our own terms, it never exists in a vacuum. Every adjustment we make affects the emotional equilibrium of those moving alongside us. Recognizing this can help us become more intentional in maintaining meaningful connection. Ask yourself:

- Where in your life might your wobble be throwing someone near you off course?
- And where might their instability be asking for a little more patience from you?

Staying aware of these subtle exchanges reminds us that balance isn't a one-time achievement. It's a living, breathing process that shifts and changes every single day.

Balance Is Impermanent, and That's Okay

What helps you find balance today, isn't what will help you achieve balance tomorrow. In fact, balance may only exist in a very small point in time, a precise point on a spectrum, like the split second on a bike when everything aligns perfectly before you lean into the next curve.

When you ride a bike, you're never still. Even when you're moving in a straight line, your handlebars shift ever so slightly, and your body responds to every bump, turn, and incline. Even when the road looks smooth, you're constantly making micro-adjustments to stay upright. Staying on the right path requires constant modification. This is *rebalancing*.

The same is true in our lives. Balance doesn't come from locking ourselves into rigid routines or unbending expectations. It comes from the willingness to notice when we're drifting, the ability to then make small corrections, and also to stay flexible in response to changing circumstances. And while that may sound exhausting at first, it's actually freeing. It means you don't have to get things perfect on the first try. You only have to stay present and responsive to the road you're currently on.

It's important to understand that balance, by its very nature, is impermanent. It is more like a fleeting point you pass through before the momentum of life carries you forward again. Like a layover in an airport, it's important but temporary. It's not meant to be the place where you stay.

The idea of a perfectly balanced life—where every moment is harmonious, every demand perfectly met, and every need effortlessly fulfilled—is a myth. Even if you touch that perfect center for a moment, it won't last. And it's not supposed to.

Balance isn't a static achievement. It's an ongoing conversation between you and your circumstances. It's not about holding one fixed position against the pressures of life. It's about learning to move with life, to flow with its inevitable shifts, and to trust yourself to make small corrections along the way.

Across work, home, and self, the balance you find today may look different than the balance you need for tomorrow. There will be times when work demands more of you, and your home life or personal life will need a little extra tending afterward to restore equilibrium. There will be times when family takes precedence, when grief, celebration, or change pulls you closer to home. There will be seasons when you need to retreat inward to tend to your own foundation of self before you can lead or serve anyone else.

Instead of chasing a flawless equilibrium, it's wiser and far more freeing, to embrace the natural shifts that happen across these areas of life. When you stop judging yourself for being "out of balance" and start paying attention to where you're tilting and why, you will gain the power to adjust before a minor lean becomes a static moment of falling over.

How can you recognize when you're tilting too far toward one pillar versus another? Think of your life as a dashboard with three main gauges or the pillars of the New Alpha: self, home, and work. Each one signals when it needs more of your balance to tip in its direction.

Signs you might be tilting too far toward work:

- You feel constantly rushed, even outside of work hours.
- Conversations with loved ones feel shallow or tense.
- You've abandoned personal practices that nourish you, like exercise, hobbies, and finding moments of stillness.

Signs you might be tilting too far toward home or relationships (at the cost of the self):

- You're ignoring your own needs to manage everyone else's emotions.
- Resentment quietly builds because you're pouring from an empty cup.
- You feel guilty any time you focus on your own growth or health.

Signs you might be tilting too far inward (at the cost of relational connection—home):

- You find yourself withdrawing from people who matter.
- Isolation starts to feel easier than communication.
- You resist new challenges or opportunities out of fear of disruption.

When you start noticing these signs, don't panic and don't criticize yourself for "failing" to find balance. Just make a small course correction. Reach out for a real conversation. Prioritize rest or play. Block off an hour to focus on your own well-being or reconnect with your work goals.

Balance is rarely lost all at once. It's also not restored all at once either. It's the accumulation of small shifts that keeps you moving forward in a way that feels stable enough for you to live as a whole person.

Managing Outside Opinions Without Losing Your Center

Knowing that balance is impermanent is helpful. But knowing won't always save you from the frustration you feel when you're wobbling in real time. Like when work stretches too long into your evenings, when home demands stack up, or when you feel judgment from others about how you're managing it all.

At various points, your colleagues, partners, friends, and children may all have opinions about whether you're in balance or not. Some of those opinions can be useful—*very* useful. Feedback from people who know you, love you, and want the best for you can reveal blind spots you can't see alone.

Other opinions, however, should be politely ignored. Not everyone's view of balance is as broad or as thoughtful as the one we're building here. And letting every outside comment destabilize you would be like trying to steer your bike by handing the handlebars to every passerby.

You need to hold your center. When feedback comes, listen carefully. Ask: *Is this helping me see something I couldn't see on my own? Is this pulling me out of alignment with what I know matters most right now?* Use discernment to decide if the feedback you're receiving is actually helpful to you or if it's coming from someone who is trying to grab your handlebars to steer your life.

Looking at the Whole Arc

Understanding balance requires us to widen the frame, especially when it comes to how we view our work lives.

It's easy to feel out of balance when deadlines stack up or when new demands are added without warning. In those moments, frustration is natural. But to evaluate balance fairly, we have to look at the whole arc, not just a single hard stretch.

Most jobs, even the demanding ones, include some built-in reprieves: holidays, personal days, conference breaks, lighter seasons, goodbye lunches, or slower periods between big projects. These moments shift the pendulum back toward the center, even if they often feel too few or too brief.

In addition to the rhythms of time off, many of us work under conditions that offer critical protections like paid sick leave, parental leave, bereavement policies, and legal job security. These are privileges not everyone around the world enjoys, and even within our own communities, not everyone has access to them. Many workers in factories, fields, mines, and service jobs—the most common jobs in America and around the globe—face different realities entirely.

Recognizing this doesn't mean you have no right to advocate for better conditions. It doesn't mean stress, burnout, or imbalance aren't real concerns. It simply means that a full, fair assessment of balance has to account for both the pressures and the protections built into *your* unique situation.

Money, too, is part of the equation. Even if it feels crass to acknowledge, the reality is that income is often exchanged for a certain level of responsibility. With that responsibility come both expectations and accommodations. Higher earning roles may demand greater sacrifice at times; they often also allow greater flexibility and autonomy and can include more long-term rewards.

This complexity of time, money, roles, and expectations is what makes navigating balance so difficult.

When I wrestled with whether to take paternity leave, for example, I wasn't only weighing days off against workload. I was confronting what it meant to lead, to provide, and to protect, not only financially, but emotionally and relationally. *How would my absence affect my team and client projects? How would my presence benefit my family?* Balancing those competing forces wasn't easy. But then again, when has balancing anything of real value ever been easy?

None of this is meant to suggest you should accept toxic, exploitative, or damaging conditions.

Nor do I want to suggest that your frustrations aren't valid or that your exhaustion isn't real. The point is simply this: If we define balance too narrowly, if we judge it by the number of hours worked in a given week, or by a single difficult project, we risk missing the bigger picture. We lose sight of the broader pattern.

To illustrate this, imagine flipping a two-sided coin. If the coin is fairly made, we can expect an even distribution of heads and tails over any number of flips. It might land on tails eight times in ten flips, making it seem as if the coin favors one side 80% of the time. But eventually it will even out. Sometimes the work of balance is simply staying present long enough to see that more balanced number (in this case, your average workload) reveal itself.

Perspective matters. Patience, reflection, and honest conversations with yourself and with others are the tools that will help you keep your balance over time—not just moment by moment, but across the whole of your life.

Seeing Balance Over Time

Balance is not a single perfect point you can freeze and hold. It's the average of many small moments of imbalance.

Sometimes you have to zoom out to see it. You may need to look across weeks or months to recognize where real balance is happening in your life. Not every season will look well-organized and tidy. Some seasons will lean more toward one pillar and farther away from another. But with time, the overall pattern of balance reveals itself.

This requires a combination of foresight and patience, both of which are easier to cultivate when you surround yourself with support. Conversations with mentors, trusted friends, or wise family members can help you expand your lens when you're stuck. So can honest self-reflection and asking better questions of yourself: *Am I drifting, or am I growing? Am I listening to fear, or to wisdom?*

It's those deeper questions that open the door to real vulnerability. The kind of vulnerability that allows you to confront where you are without self-judgment and to be seen by others—imperfections, wobbles, and all. So with those things in mind, let's next talk about vulnerability and how we can use it as a source of strength and leadership while cultivating balance across all areas of our lives.

Chapter 7

Practicing Emotional Leadership

He who conquers others is strong; he who
conquers himself is mighty.
–Lao Tzu, *Tao Te Ching*

The Warmth-Competence Equation

You might think most people follow leaders who appear invincible. Research tells a different story. In an article published in *Harvard Business Review*, psychologist Amy Cuddy states that people decide whether to trust you based on two things: your warmth and your competence.[10] Dominant traits like the perception of invincibility, power, and control have nothing to do with it. Surprisingly, between warmth and competence, warmth comes first. This is because before people care how much you know or how well you can perform, they need to know one thing: *Do I feel safe with you?*

---

10   Amy J. C. Cuddy, Matthew Kohut, John Neffinger, "Connect, Then Lead," *Harvard Business Review* (2013), https://hbr.org/2013/07/connect-then-lead.

To effectively lead others, you must understand and balance the warmth-competence dynamic. If you're seen as competent but not warm, you may earn respect but also resentment; if you're warm but not competent, you might get sympathy but not real influence or respect. Many leaders default to showcasing strength and credentials first, and that approach often backfires. Leading with strength before trust can trigger fear, which stifles creativity, problem-solving, and engagement.

Cuddy's research shows that the most effective path to influence and leadership is to start with warmth. Even small signals of openness, like smiling, build trust quickly. These signals make people feel seen and understood. It shows them it's safe to engage with you.

For many, this dynamic may feel unnatural. Most of us are taught to lead by projecting competence and demanding control of the room. Warmth has always been optional. For some of us, because it didn't feel essential, warmth never even entered the equation in our professional lives.

It felt a bit unnatural when I learned this and started incorporating more warmth into my leadership dynamic. I have a dry sense of humor. I enjoy it, and I enjoy it in others; but I was taught not to be a clown. I was taught to be serious. and I took that to heart. I still see the value in that posture. At the start of my career, connection used to feel like a byproduct, not something I prioritized. But over time I came to understand its importance as a gateway to meaningful dialogue and leadership. The conversation with my Harvard professor that I mentioned in chapter 4 helped enforce this shift. Knowing that her opinion of me improved after she learned of my desire to connect with others illustrates Cuddy's research that connection comes before intelligence, competence, or any other factor.

Knowing this, I learned to lead more openly. I started using more words when I was frustrated, instead of giving off a tone. I learned when to say less and when to share more. I let people see more of me—not everything, but enough—because that's what builds trust and connection. I smile a lot more now than I ever used to, especially with folks in the customer service space. And I've noticed how even something as small as that can shift the dynamic immediately. That smile disarms people and invites them in.

It takes courage to invite connection without knowing how it will be received. That willingness lays the groundwork for a new kind of leadership, one that's rooted in emotional presence. To fully understand why that matters, we have to look at the model that many of us were handed.

Diagnosing the Old Model

Many of us were raised inside a model of strength that valued composure over connection. We were taught that to be a man meant to be a leader, and to be a leader meant to suppress what was soft and to overdevelop what was sharp. Vulnerability, empathy, even emotional language itself was treated as suspect.

The model worked, until it didn't. At some point, this model left us overperforming and disconnected. Relationships started to crack under the weight of everything we weren't saying.

This isn't only a man's issue; it's a reflection of deeper cultural conditioning that's impacted how everyone shows up in leadership. The emotional burden of the old model has spilled across gender lines, shaping the professional expectations for both men and women.

A 2003 study in the American Psychologist[11] examines how women in leadership often feel pressure to adopt traditionally masculine traits, like assertiveness, competitiveness, and dominance to succeed. This can backfire due to persistent gender role expectations. The pressure to "lead like a man" can create internal conflict and contribute to burnout or inauthentic leadership styles that aren't necessarily effective or sustainable.

Studies show this double-bind clearly—it's a no-win situation where any choice a woman makes comes with a penalty. Women who lead with assertiveness are seen as competent but unlikable. Those who lead with too much warmth are liked, but underestimated. It's a lose-lose when the model itself is broken. The adoption of these "masculine" traits doesn't always serve women well; they often must walk a tightrope between warmth and strength.

Another study applied Gender Role Conflict theory[12] to women who adopt traits such as emotional restriction, success obsession, and aggressive competition. The study found that these masculine traits can lead to stress, dissatisfaction, and

---

11   Alice H. Eagly and Linda L. Carli, "The Female Leadership Advantage: An Evaluation of the Evidence," *American Psychologist,* 58, no.2, (2003):110–117.

12   John M. O'Neil and Marcia Harway, "A Multivariate Model Explaining Gender Role Conflict in Women, *Psychology of Women Quarterly,* 21, no. 3 (1997): 345–364.

compromised relationships when they conflict with women's values or social expectations.

Some feminist analyses[13] argue that in response to male-dominated environments, some women adopt combative or hypercompetitive behaviors that mirror toxic masculinity. These behaviors may reflect a coping mechanism rather than empowerment and often undermine collaboration, empathy, and inclusivity.

The irony is, the very traits leaders have been taught to suppress—like openness, empathy, and emotional fluency—are the ones that build trust with teams, create safety at home, and keep us in relationship with ourselves. And yet, because they don't look like dominance, and we've misdefined leadership as dominance, we've treated these traits as liabilities instead of leadership assets.

What we need is a deeper reckoning. If the traits we've long dismissed are the very ones that sustain connection, maybe it's not only our definition of leadership that needs to change but our definition of strength itself.

Redefining Leadership's Role to Emphasize the Protective Element

For generations, men were taught that their role was to protect. But the threats we're facing now aren't always outside of us the way they have been for most of humanity's existence. Rather than wolves outside our village, modern threats live in the

---

13   Carol Gilligan, *In a Different Voice: Psychological Theory and Women's Development*, (Cambridge, MA: Harvard University Press 1993; originally published 1982).

tension of our relationships, the disconnection in our homes, and the burnout we carry silently.

Leadership has always been associated with the ability to protect. In early human societies, leaders were often the strongest and most capable individuals who could ensure the group's survival by providing resources like food and shelter—and protecting the groups they served from external dangers. But as societies grew and became more complex, leaders became individuals with skills in areas like managing resources, maintaining social order, and providing conflict resolution. This form of leadership was rooted in service to the community, where the leader's authority stemmed from their ability to perform critical tasks benefiting the group.

Aggression was no longer the key trait of a competent leader. Yes, aggression can defend against an outside threat. But empathy defends against collapse from within. Modern leaders are still expected to protect their tribes by protecting their team's well-being, defending the interests of those on the teams, and helping them develop resilience to cope with challenges and demands. If we're going to be protectors, we have to protect the emotional and psychological safety of the people we care about. That includes our partners, our children, our teams, and ourselves.

We know that the old model of leadership no longer meets the expectation of modern leadership. If the old model is broken, the definition must evolve.

It's possible to protect someone's body and still harm their spirit—to provide materially while the emotional needs go unmet. You can occupy the same room but still feel oceans apart from the people in it.

That shift in how we define protection shows up in the smallest choices. We may think we're protecting our loved ones by keeping stress from work out of the house or that disappearing into overwork is a noble way to provide. To an outside observer, that absence feels like neglect.

This is what makes the modern protector role more nuanced and more demanding. It's not enough to shield your family from the world. You also have to shield them from the parts of you that were taught to disconnect, suppress, and compartmentalize.

The old model says, "Take the hit so they don't have to." The new model says, "Do the work so they don't inherit your wounds."

Protection, in this reimagined context, looks like emotional availability. It's asking your child how they're doing and waiting for the real answer, not just their automated response. Or it's modeling vulnerability so your partner feels safe to bring their whole, honest self to the relationship and doesn't feel obligated to put up walls that mirror your own.

We're not aiming to eliminate the warrior archetype when we reevaluate the protector role. We're transforming it to be more suitable in the modern world. We're molding it into something deeper. We're reframing it so it's no longer only about shielding those around us, but also about cultivating a safe and nurturing environment.

As we move beyond the traditional roles and redefine what it means to protect and lead, it's time to look at the next layer of this work: how we show up emotionally.

Becoming an Emotional Leader

Here I want to introduce a concept called Emotional Leadership. This is where your behavior stays true to yourself, and you remain yourself in any situation without regard to thinking or wondering how someone else might view you as a person. It's where you embody confidence by knowing that what you bring to the table is sufficient, even if you're not immediately understood by others.

Emotional leadership does not mean you need to overexplain, overaccommodate, or constantly manage emotional responses of others at the expense of your own clarity or boundaries. It means you're no longer dependent on the temperature of the room to decide how you'll show up in it. You act from a space grounded in your own clarity. It means guiding your relationships, teams, and families with presence, awareness, and authenticity.

Being more of yourself and allowing that to come through— especially in moments where it would be easier to choose performative behavior—creates a connection that opens the door for the people around you to exhale and do the same.

In leadership, that's a massive advantage. It allows you to guide conversations instead of reacting to them. It helps you ask better questions. But more than anything, it helps people trust that who you are in public is the same as who you are in private.

That kind of steadiness is rare and it's admired. When people feel that authenticity in you, they'll follow.

Emotional leadership is about showing up whole. It's what allows you to lead without needing to dominate and to connect without needing to perform. At its core, it asks something of you that isn't always easy: the courage to be vulnerable, even if you are the first one to take down your guard.

Practicing Vulnerability in Leadership

It's one thing to understand that vulnerability is powerful. It's another thing to practice it, especially in environments where you haven't always felt safe.

For most of my life, I didn't associate vulnerability with strength. Like a lot of men, I filed it somewhere under "exposure." Vulnerability made me feel naked and unsafe. But over time, I've learned that real strength begins with honesty, and honesty requires vulnerability. If you can't be honest with yourself, if you can't acknowledge what's not working, there's no way to change anything. Vulnerability is what opens the door to change and deepens connection with our partners, our children, and our teams.

When you lead with vulnerability, you're putting the warmth-competence equation into action. As Cuddy's research shows, people respond to warmth before they ever assess your skill set. Vulnerability demonstrates warmth because it signals openness, humanity, and trust. It also reinforces competence since it takes grounded self-awareness and emotional maturity to lead from your truth rather than your image.

Leadership is the ability to show up with clarity, integrity, and emotional presence, whether or not the room is ready for you. It involves modeling what it looks like to stay rooted in your values while making space for others to do the same. Real leadership starts within. If I'm not grounded in who I am, if I haven't taken the time to check in with myself, then whatever I bring into a room, a relationship, a company, or a family is going to reflect that lack of clarity.

That's the hardest part of vulnerability, especially for men who've been told our power comes from certainty. It asks you to go first. It asks you to say the thing without knowing how it will be received and to know that showing up with your full self is what is going to cultivate trust.

Becoming vulnerable is not something you can shift into overnight. It's not like you're putting on a new identity like a costume you can zip up in the mirror. It's going to take years. You may see some change right away, but overall, it is going to be slow.

How to Practice Vulnerability in Real Life

Below are tangible ways to begin practicing emotional leadership by embracing vulnerability as a daily habit.

1. Start Small and Be Specific

You don't have to spill your life story to be vulnerable. Begin with micro-moments of honesty:

- Say, "I'm not sure" when you don't know.
- Let your facial expressions reflect what you actually feel.

- Share when you're feeling off, tired, overwhelmed, or uncertain.

These honest disclosures build relational safety over time. Starting small builds the internal muscle of emotional courage. When you take the steps to build that emotional foundation, moments like admitting a mistake at work or opening up about burnout don't feel so destabilizing because you've already practiced showing up with integrity instead of defense.

2. Seek Safe Spaces

Find people who can hold space for what you're sharing without trying to fix your problems or who turn away from you because of what you're saying.

This might be a brother or a friend who listens without judgement. It could be a mentor, someone who has walked a similar path as you and understands what you've been through and knows where you're going. It might be a therapist, especially if you've spent years wearing the same stoic mask and find it difficult to remove it.

Some of my most important leadership breakthroughs started in therapy sessions where no one else was watching—where I was just a man learning how to speak plainly. Therapists and coaches are trained to hold emotional space to help you build tools like emotional language, self-awareness, regulation, and communication, so you can show up more clearly and courageously in every part of your life.

No matter who you turn to, what matters most is that you feel safe enough to be honest and supported enough to keep moving forward in your growth.

3. Practice Self-Compassion

As you practice becoming your own version of the New Alpha, you will miss the mark sometimes. You might snap at your partner or kids after a long day at work, even though you promised to be more patient at home. You might find yourself micromanaging your team and defaulting to control at work rather than leading from a place of trust. Or you might push yourself to burnout because rest still feels unfamiliar. When these moments occur, it's important to practice self-compassion. This part of the journey is slow. Some days you'll speak up with courage. Other days you'll pull back. What matters is that you keep showing up. Leadership doesn't require emotional perfection; it does require consistency. And the more we model honest, grounded leadership in action, the more we invite others to do the same.

The New Alpha as an Emotional Leader

True leadership is no longer defined by dominance or control. It is the ability to lead with emotional intelligence, vulnerability, and warmth. These qualities have been proven to build trust, deepen connection, and create lasting impact circles of influence.

To embody this kind of leadership, we must dismantle the old model that equated strength with suppression. We have to redefine protection to include room for emotional availability.

Whether we're at home, at work, or alone with ourselves, leadership means taking responsibility for the energy we bring into every space. That's why the New Alpha leads from emotional integrity—not from a perceived image of perfection or from control.

You won't get it right every time. But if you're willing to go first, as leaders do, you give others permission to do the same. That's how we begin to change not only how we lead, but how we live.

Emotional leadership starts with how we show up for others and it's sustained by how we show up for ourselves. In the next chapter, we'll zoom in on the internal world and discuss how to reconnect with yourself and build a healthier inner voice that supports your growth instead of sabotaging it.

Chapter 8

Reconnecting With Oneself

Know thyself.
–Inscription at the Temple of Apollo at Delphi

How High Expectations Can Create Inner Disconnection

The first clue that I needed to reconnect with myself started with something so small it almost escaped my notice. I noticed I was increasingly annoyed with people who were slow to respond to my messages or didn't respond at all, even within a day or two. I realized that the people who annoyed me the most were the ones I called my closest friends.

In order to understand why the slow replies were bothering me, I had to put the situation in context. I thought about the nature of my relationships, how long I'd known these friends, the value they brought to my life, and our shared history. When I looked at it that way, I realized my frustration wasn't really about them. It came from the fact that I personally placed a high value on being responsive. I responded quickly to messages and always within the same day. If I was going to bed and realized that somebody sent me a message and I hadn't responded, I wouldn't go to sleep until I replied. Quick responsiveness was my personal standard, not necessarily the standard of my friends. And yet I held them to the same high expectations I required of myself.

I realized that no one else expected this same response rate, though my friends may have become used to it. When I realized this, I also recognized that if I were to lighten up on myself or remove this standard by giving myself more leniency in response time, my impatience and frustration with others would also lessen. When I did this, my friends' delays stopped bothering me. I still noticed them, but I no longer took them personally. The tension lifted.

That was the moment I began to understand something deeper: Much of my frustration with others came from the way I treated myself. The strict expectations, the constant sense of urgency, even my inner self-criticism was leaking into my relationships.

Around that time, I came across an article about anger. This was over a decade ago, and I no longer remember the title of the article, but its contents spurred an important shift in my life. The article was about how to notice and reduce anger. It explored how we often carry resentment not because others have truly wronged us, but because their actions highlight an internal imbalance—some unmet expectation we're clinging to often without realizing it.

I started seeing other examples in my life. There were moments where I'd felt anger or judgment toward someone else, only to realize it was because they hadn't acted the way I would have. But who said they had to?

When I decided to turn judgment into curiosity, and expectations into empathy, my life shifted. And yes, that shift helped to improve my relationship with others; at the core, it was about reconnecting with myself. Developing empathy towards others allowed me to have a greater degree of empathy with myself. I realized that self-awareness is a mirror. I saw how tightly I was holding myself, how rigid my standards were, and how quickly I turned small lapses into self-criticism. By easing my stance toward others, I gave myself permission to ease my inward stance toward myself too.

That one moment of self-awareness—sparked by something as mundane as a delayed reply—showed me how tightly I was holding myself to arbitrary standards and how that pressure was bleeding into my opinion of those around me.

But noticing the problem was only the first step. The deeper work came in understanding where these unconscious thought patterns came from and why they had taken root in the first place. Before I could reconnect with myself, I first had to recognize that I had become disconnected from myself.

Disconnection Always Comes First

Disconnection is when the way you live no longer reflects who you truly are. It happens when your behaviors, thoughts, or choices drift out of alignment with your values, your emotional truth, or the needs of the people who matter most to you—including yourself.

No one is born disconnected. Children are naturally connected to themselves. They think and feel freely. They haven't yet learned to suppress emotions, perform roles, or filter their truth through social approval. Children aren't yet trained to "behave," to hide emotions, or to prioritize politeness over authenticity.

Disconnection is learned. It's a necessary but sometimes overextended adaptation to function in a structured society. Children begin in a state of internal congruence: their thoughts, feelings, and actions are aligned with who they truly are. But over time, expectations, external pressures, and unexamined rules pull them out of that state.

Becoming a polite, socially acceptable adult often requires some level of disconnection between what you feel and what you express, between what you want and how you behave. Some of that is reasonable. You can't act on every impulse or feeling without consequences; a functioning society depends on some degree of self-restraint. The problem is when that restraint becomes the default. It's when you forget how to listen inwardly at all. That's when disconnection stops being a helpful social tool and starts becoming a habit that cuts you off from your core self.

Now that you've become aware of disconnection, you may notice signs of it in your own life. This can look like burnout, emotional numbness, chronic dissatisfaction, unfulfilling relationships, or imbalance across the different domains of your life, especially among the core pillars of work, home, and self.

Left unexamined, disconnection tends to compound. The longer you go without turning inward, the wider the gap between how you act and who you truly are. If you're heavily influenced by what's happening around you and by what other people or society expect of you—and you haven't done any real introspection to determine who you actually are or how you want to live—then it becomes easy to lose touch with your core self entirely. But it doesn't have to stay that way.

What It Means to Reconnect

Reconnecting with yourself means realigning your actions, thoughts, and values with your core self. Who you truly are lies beneath the roles and expectations you've been taught to adopt. Reconnecting with yourself is the process of becoming intentional again. It's noticing where you've drifted away from your innate self and taking the action to come back to that core version of you.

To do that you must provide an honest evaluation to determine the parts of you that have been neglected and at what cost. Maybe you've been pouring everything into work while ignoring your physical health. Maybe you've shown up for everyone else but haven't had a real conversation with yourself in months. Disconnection isn't always visible to outside eyes, and often it's not even immediately visible to yourself. It can show up as exhaustion, emotional numbness, or a nagging sense that something's off. These signs are easy to miss if you're not looking for them, and they're even easier to normalize if you don't take the time to ask why those signs are showing up.

To reconnect, it helps to ask:

- What have I been overvaluing in my life? Is it productivity, control, perfection, or being needed? And for what purpose? Do I value these things to feel worthy, to feel safe, or to avoid failure and discomfort?
- What have I been sacrificing for the sake of achievement, approval, survival, or simply keeping up?

Reconnection begins by recognizing the misalignment in yourself and deciding you're no longer willing to live at the expense of your own well-being. In my case, that meant questioning the values I thought were nonnegotiable.

I remember walking with a friend one evening as he talked about his hopes for his children. He said, "All I want is for them to fulfill their potential." At one point, I would've said the same. But in that moment, I realized that was no longer true for me. I no longer believed that was the goal.

What I really want for my child, and for myself, is to feel fulfilled. To contribute, to grow, but not through exhaustion at the cost of joy. There are plenty of people who've "fulfilled their potential" and are completely miserable.

That realization was a form of reconnection. It required me to challenge the beliefs I'd inherited and decide what I actually value, not just what I've been taught to chase. I'm now learning to balance the question of my potential—what it is, where it lies, and how to use it—in a way that's honest, challenging, and well-examined. I want to offer the greatest good to the greatest number of people without sacrificing so much of myself that I end up exhausted and miserable. And the last thing I want to do is undermine the very greatness I'm trying to achieve.

Reconnecting with yourself starts with redefining what truly matters to you, and then having the courage to live in alignment with that truth.

How to Begin Reconnecting

Once you've recognized the disconnection, the next step is creating space to come back to yourself. Reconnecting with yourself is a truly personal exercise. It's not about comparing your pace to others or feeling behind because you haven't hit certain milestones. If anything, it's more useful to look to people who seem grounded—who carry calm, clarity, and order in their lives—and study how they've cultivated that.

One way to start reconnecting is to ask yourself some honest questions:

- Whose goals am I pursuing?
- Whose life am I living?
- Who have I impacted along the way?
- What do I care about?
- What kind of man do I want to be?
- Am I living in alignment with my values?
- When it's all said and done, how satisfied will I be with what I've achieved and how I've achieved it?

Sometimes disconnection shows up as chasing one thing after another, seeking approval, feeling emotionally flat, or achieving milestone after milestone and still feeling empty. You may sacrifice yourself and those closest to you in the process without even realizing it. Often, others reflect that disconnection back to you. If you're frequently misunderstood, ignored, or misaligned in your relationships, it might not be about them. It could be a sign that something in *you* is out of sync.

Self-care is one of the most accessible ways to begin the process of reconnection. This might look like journaling, meditating, exercising, stretching, spending time in nature, practicing your spirituality, or preparing your own meals. Whether it's movement, stillness, reflection, or nourishment, self-care comes in many forms.

Therapy can also be a powerful part of the reconnection process. A skilled therapist helps you unpack the patterns you can't always see on your own, offering both clarity and compassion as you rediscover your inner voice.

When you carve out time to meet your physical and emotional needs, you're already beginning to come home to yourself. Simply acknowledging yourself for showing up in these small ways can help rebuild self-trust.

Reconnecting with yourself isn't something that happens all at once. It's not like running into an old friend at the grocery store and quickly catching up. Because you're with yourself all the time, you can actually stop *really* seeing yourself. Just like with anything else you're constantly exposed to, you can become desensitized.

That's why reconnection requires intentionality. You won't accidentally run into yourself; you have to meet yourself on purpose. That might mean blocking off time in your calendar, creating a routine, or choosing a physical space where you can pause and reflect. But the goal is the same: to create space where you can actually see yourself again.

Building a Healthy Internal Voice

Of course, none of these practices will take root unless you're also paying attention to how you speak to yourself when no one else is listening.

I don't know exactly when I became aware of my inner voice. I don't think most people notice that initial moment of awareness. I also don't think it's something we're born with. I believe that voice has to be developed. It starts to form once societal expectations get foisted on us. And depending on what we heard most, whether discipline, encouragement, shame, or love; that's what the voice inside us begins to echo.

Our inner voice is, at first, a recollection. Over time, it takes on a life of its own. It starts to dictate how we operate, sometimes so subtly that we don't even realize it. Like a form of artificial intelligence, it's built on inputs we didn't choose. The things we experienced, the feedback we received, the lessons we internalized—all of the shapes voice can take—the nature, tone, frequency, and intensity.

If we weren't spoken to with care, or if we continue placing ourselves in environments that reinforce harshness, it's easy for that voice to turn cruel. If you didn't grow up with nurturing voices around you, you still have the opportunity, and maybe even the obligation, to re-parent yourself. Audit that voice and ask: *Is this mine? Is it helping me? Is it fair and caring?*

The way we talk to ourselves matters more than we often realize. For a long time, I held myself to rigid internal standards. At the time I thought of it as being a responsible adult. Eventually I saw how harsh my inner dialogue had become. There wasn't much room for grace. I constantly judged and measured myself against what I hadn't done yet.

What I came to realize was when the voice you live with is sharp and demeaning, you start projecting it outward. My frustration with others was often a mirror of how tightly I was holding myself. Reconnecting with myself meant shifting that inner voice from self-judgment to self-compassion. I realized that if I couldn't extend empathy inward to myself, I'd always struggle to extend it to anyone else.

Ask yourself: If *my inner voice spoke to my loved ones the way it speaks to me, how would they respond? Would they feel encouraged? Respected? Safe? Or would they walk away feeling small, ashamed, or misunderstood? Would I be proud of that voice or embarrassed by it?*

One thing I've realized is how rarely we offer ourselves the same patience we extend to others. I hadn't even considered that until recently. Several months ago, I had a conversation with a friend of mine who had been sober for eight months after struggling with alcohol. But one night, he slipped. When I saw him, he was frustrated and disappointed with himself. He told me he felt like he'd failed completely. I reminded him: "You're not in a race. You're not competing with anyone—not even the days on a calendar. It's not that you lost an eight-month streak. It's that you went eight whole months and only drank once." That's progress worth celebrating.

As I said these words to my friend, I wondered, *How often have I offered that kind of grace to myself?*

If we can begin speaking to ourselves in the gentle, honest, and encouraging way we speak to a friend, it would transform more than our mood. It would reshape our relationship to ourselves and to those around us. There's a ripple effect that radiates outward, because when we're more patient and honest with ourselves, we become more vulnerable with others. We admit mistakes and we acknowledge imperfections, and those very admissions create connection.

You may not know it, but our weaknesses usually aren't secrets. The people who know us well also know our flaws. They see us trying to hide them like we're wearing a bad toupee. Everyone knows when those issues are there, and that draws more attention to what you're trying to cover.

When we own our struggles, we become more relatable. People admire leaders who've had setbacks and have grown from them. They're inspired not only by what we've achieved, but by what we've overcome.

So yes, how you speak to yourself matters. That inner voice influences your sense of self-worth, your authenticity, and your integrity. And as it was shaped through repetition and reinforcement over the years, it can also be reshaped. You can reorient that voice.

How Self-Connection Changes Every Relationship

Reconnecting with yourself doesn't only change how you feel internally, it also changes how you show up in your relationship with others. When you start releasing rigid expectations and harsh self-judgment, your relationships often begin to shift as well.

Once I gave myself permission to ease up on my messaging response time, I found that my judgment toward others softened too. That shift in how I treated myself allowed me to show up with more grace in my friendships.

That's the ripple effect of self-connection. When you're more patient and forgiving with yourself, you naturally become more patient and forgiving with others. You stop expecting people to live up to the standards you hold yourself to, especially when those standards were never compassionate to begin with.

Reconnection fosters empathy. The more honest and accepting you are toward your own imperfections, the more room you create for others to be fully human too. And in that space, relationships deepen, trust grows, and connection with others becomes more authentic.

In the next chapter, we'll explore what that outward connection really looks like. Then we'll discuss how to reconnect with family, lead with emotional intelligence at work, and rebuild relationships that may have been strained by old patterns.

Chapter 9

Reconnection With Others

No man is an island, entire of itself; every man is a piece
of the continent, a part of the main.
–JOHN DONNE, *Devotions upon Emergent Occasions,*
Meditation 17 (1624)

Why Reconnection Matters

The first time I can remember being truly vulnerable in a conversation was with my brother. It was 1995, and he was in the hospital. We were trying to figure out what was wrong with him. One morning, before school, we were all leaving after a visit. Everyone had already started walking away, but I paused. I turned back around and said, "I love you."

He was 10; I was 17 at the time. He nodded at me and sort of smiled, like he was saying, "Okay." I smiled back at him and then left for school. I'm grateful I stopped to say that because that was the last time I ever spoke to him.

That moment has always stayed with me. It was one of the first times I acted on the instinct to be vulnerable, and I've never regretted it. Any time I've felt that something needed to be said—*really said*—and I listened to that inner voice, I've been glad I did.

Not too long before my brother died, my father started leading us in a family exercise where we would go around the room and say "I love you" to everybody. It felt awkward and a bit unnatural at first because those words weren't something we were accustomed to saying, especially in a formal drill like that. But now the words come much easier to me than they did when I was a teenager. I now often tell my parents that I love them, and I also make a point to say it to my friends, both the guys and the women.

It was from these moments in my later teens that I learned how vulnerability is essential to forming strong relationships. The courage to share how you feel creates the conditions for trust, empathy, and emotional intimacy. Without vulnerability, people may coexist but remain disconnected and unable to truly see or be seen by one another.

Looking back I realize that what I was learning—even if I didn't have the words for it yet—was emotional literacy. Emotional literacy is the ability to recognize, understand, express, and manage your own emotions while also being attuned to the emotions of others. It's a skill set that helps you navigate relationships with empathy and clarity.

When we talk about reconnecting with others, we're not only talking about repairing a broken relationship. We're talking about choosing to show up emotionally, however scary or awkward that may feel at first, and reengage in relationships with honesty. This is especially important in contexts where emotional literacy hasn't always been modeled.

It's our relationships that shape how we experience life. Because of that, our relationships are central to all three pillars. It's the people we're connected to who influence how we see ourselves, how we show up for our family and friends, and how we lead. When our relationships are strained, that disconnection doesn't stay contained in one area; it bleeds out across the other pillars. Without connection, even our achievements can feel hollow.

Reconnection is also at the heart of effective leadership. Whether you're leading a family, a team, or trying to show up more fully in your friendships, the quality of your relationships will determine the quality of your impact. Emotional literacy builds trust, opens doors to deeper understanding, and helps us create the kind of environments where people actually feel supported and safe.

And the reason reconnection with others matters is that it restores the trust and closeness we need to feel seen. Without that, even our strongest efforts—at work, at home, or within ourselves—can feel empty. We're wired for connection, and when it's missing, our sense of meaning and belonging begins to wear away. Reconnection with others gives us the foundation to thrive. Like reconnecting with ourselves, in order to reconnect with others, we must first identify that there is some sort of disconnection to begin with.

Defining Disconnection With Others

Disconnection with others often manifests through a lack of trust. It appears when you start to wonder if the people around you have your best interests at heart. You notice it when you begin to ask yourself if you can be honest with the people in your life. Do they care about who you are, not just what you do?

When the answers to these questions are unclear, it's natural to pull back and create distance in the relationship. You might be physically around people yet no longer attuned to them. It can look like strained communication, unresolved tension, or simply going through the motions. Sometimes it shows up as silence or formality where there used to be easy communication.

Disconnection doesn't always stem from conflict. Often it's the result of unspoken expectations or a lack of intentionality. It can happen in families, in marriages, at work, and in friendships. Sometimes we don't even notice disconnection is there until it's taken root and we suddenly realize we're no longer being fully honest or engaged with the people who matter most.

At home, disconnection can look like emotional detachment, being in the same room but no longer truly curious about each other's lives. At work, it might show up when leaders care more about output than people. It's hard to stay engaged when someone stops showing interest in your growth or your goals, or you start to feel like a cog in the machine. You may still perform what you're required to do, but you're not bringing your full self to the table.

A big part of the challenge is that we tend to judge others by their actions and ourselves by our intentions. So even if you meant well, if you don't express that intention or back it up with consistent behavior, people's trust in you will break down.

At its core, disconnection is what happens when trust erodes and we're no longer emotionally invested in each other's well-being. Without that foundation, vulnerability and emotional reciprocity fade away.

How to Begin to Reconnect With Others

To begin to reconnect with those around you, there has to first be an acknowledgement that something isn't operating as well as it could. Once you realize that there is room for improvement in your relationships, then you have to be willing to move towards that improvement. That acknowledgement is the first step toward change.

This is a book about leadership, so of course reconnection has a leadership component. But showing up as a leader in your relationships doesn't require a title or official role. While people in formal leadership positions (parents, managers, and community leaders) have a responsibility to set the tone for trust and to create space for honest dialogue, emotional leadership belongs to anyone in any kind of relationship. Whether you're a teen talking to a parent, a friend reaching out, or a team member at work—if you're a human with human relationships, it is in your domain to initiate reconnection. Reconnection is relational, and both sides hold the power to improve it.

As for how to initiate reconnection, there's no single blueprint to follow. Initiating reconnection will look different for everyone, depending on the context, the people involved, and the dynamics at play. What follows are some reflections and practices that I've drawn from my own experience. These are the ways I've approached reconnection at home with family, at work, and in the communities I'm part of.

Remembering the Traits of Connection

Some of the most powerful tools we have for initiating reconnection are things we already know and simply need to remember. There is a growing body of psychological research suggesting that people who report strong feelings of connection often exhibit qualities like playfulness, curiosity, emotional honesty, and awe. These traits come naturally to us as children but are often subdued when we transition into adulthood.

Psychologists have long shown that positive emotions like joy and playfulness expand our awareness and build stronger social bonds. American researcher Barbara L. Fredrickson's broaden-and-build theory of positive emotions suggests that playful states open us up to deeper connection and emotional resilience.[14] Playfulness in this sense becomes more than a fun mood, as it actually creates a doorway to connection. Studies have found that adults who intentionally bring playfulness into their relationships experience more satisfaction and closeness

---

14   Barbara L. Fredrickson, "The Role of Positive Emotions in Positive Psychology: The Broaden-and-Build Theory of Positive Emotions," *American Psychologist* 56 no. 3 (2001): 218–226.

over time.[15] Being willing to act silly or look ridiculous signals a sense of safety in the home and disrupts the rigid roles we often fall into when life becomes routine.

The same is true for presence and curiosity, both of which are innate to children and essential for reconnection. Mindfulness research shows that being present in the moment not only reduces stress but also increases empathy and attunement to others.[16] That presence allows us to notice what's going on beneath the surface of a conversation. In the same vein, a 2020 study in *The Journal of Positive Psychology* found that people with higher levels of curiosity reported deeper relationships and a stronger sense of belonging in their communities.[17] Curiosity keeps us from assuming we know everything about the people closest to us, and it shows them that we're interested in what is happening in their lives.

Vulnerability is perhaps the most essential trait of all. As American academic and storyteller Brené Brown's research has shown, vulnerability is the birthplace of connection. We build connections with those who allow themselves to be seen without feeling shame, creating stronger and more meaningful bonds.[18] It's a skill we often suppress in adulthood for fear of judgement, but in truth, it's what creates the conditions for

---

15   R. T. Proyer "A New Structural Model for Adult Playfulness: Assessment and Exploration of an Understudied Individual Differences Variable," *Personality and Individual Differences,* 108 (2017): 113–122.

16   Jon Kabat-Zinn,. "Mindfulness-Based Interventions in Context: Past, Present, and Future," *Clinical Psychology: Science and Practice,* 10 no.2 (2003): 144–156.

17   Todd B. Kashdan and Paul E. McKnight, "The Curiosity Advantage: How Curiosity Enhances Social Relationships," *The Journal of Positive Psychology,* 15 no. 5 (2020): 605–614.

18   Brené Brown, *Daring Greatly: How the Courage to Be Vulnerable Transforms the Way We Live, Love, Parent, and Lead,* (New York: Gotham Books 2012).

trust. Vulnerability disarms defensiveness and invites the other person to lower their guard too. Secure attachment, the foundation of healthy relationships, is built not on perfection but on consistent emotional transparency and mutual care.

Even the feeling of awe has been found to increase empathy and promote unity. When we encounter something vast or beautiful and allow ourselves to feel small in its presence, our attention shifts away from the self and toward others.[19] That shift matters, especially in relationships where pride or self-protection can keep us disconnected. Awe reminds us of our shared humanity and helps soften the edges around long-held emotional defenses. It reminds us that we're part of something bigger than ourselves, which helps put our personal fears, ego, or grievances into a wider, more balanced view.

This research shows that people who feel the most connected to others often embody childlike qualities like openness, play, presence, emotional honesty, and wonder. These traits dismantle the emotional barriers that foster disconnection and create the space where reconnection can actually take root.

Reconnecting With Older Generations

Reconnecting with others often starts by reclaiming the emotional openness we naturally had as children. But what happens when we try to bring those qualities into relationships with people who were never taught to value them? Particularly with older generations of men (like fathers, uncles, and mentors), we may find ourselves reaching across a cultural

---

19   Paul K. Piff et al., "Awe, the Small Self, and Prosocial Behavior," *Journal of Personality and Social Psychology*, 108 no. 6 (2015): 883–899.

and emotional gap. Many of the older men in our lives were raised in environments where emotional literacy wasn't modeled, let alone encouraged. As a result, these are some of the relationships most likely to suffer from disconnection, and yet they're some of the most important relationships we have.

When initiating reconnection in relationships like these, we can start by thinking about who these people are and how they communicate. For many of these men open communication, if it happened at all, was usually for functional purposes only. So when we attempt to engage in more open, emotionally honest conversations, we have to start by thinking carefully about the context. What was their background and history of communication like before entering into the connection-based conversation?

Sometimes the most effective way to open that dialog is by naming your own growth. By saying, "Here's something I've been working on…" or, "I've realized I need to be more patient, more communicative, a little more gentle…" you can create space for the other person to open up. You're not telling them what they need to do, you're offering your own example. And even if vulnerability isn't their native language, they will usually understand what you're attempting to do.

In these moments, curiosity goes a long way. In addition to sharing what you've been working on, you can prompt them to share something about their lives. You don't have to make a grand speech. Sometimes by asking, "What were things like for you growing up?" or "What did you learn about being a man from your dad?" you can open up emotional honesty without forcing it.

There's also value in making slow changes. You don't always need to dive straight into an emotional conversation and try to change everything at once. Sometimes it's more effective to approach things subtly—by raising a topic, making an observation, or sharing something that shows you're thinking differently about masculinity or mental health. These small signals can challenge old norms and model a more open way of relating. Sometimes something as simple as sitting beside them, watching a game, or joking around can create the opening. Playfulness might seem small, but it signals safety. It reminds them of simpler times, and that they can let their guard down around you. In that sense, you're reconnecting through example rather than direct confrontation.

Sometimes, when the relationship allows for it, it's worth gently questioning the moment. If someone makes a snide or dismissive comment, you can pause and say, "Why do you think that is?" or "Have you ever felt that way yourself?" Asking these questions opens up an invitation for them to think about the comments they're making and maybe have a conversation about it. In honest relationships, people will often open up. It doesn't always happen, but sometimes it does. And working to set up that opportunity is worth the effort in either case.

Encouraging Open Conversation

In my own experience, vulnerability tends to show up late. It's usually when illness begins to manifest, along with the fear that there is limited time left. It's during this time that people finally start saying what they've been wanting to say for years. It's in hospital beds where people will finally share the things they never shared because they didn't know how, were afraid of being judged, or were scared of hurting someone they care about. But it doesn't have to take a health scare or a hospital visit to get to that conversation. We can reverse engineer the moment by asking this question right now: "If this were our last conversation, what would you want to tell me?"

There are tools that can help make this easier. I've found conversation starter games to be surprisingly powerful. You can pull a few questions from the deck or go through them together, letting the prompts guide the other person into telling stories you've never heard, all while you share parts of your life they may not expect. More than anything, these tools help shift the center of gravity in the relationship, gently rekindling a connection that may have faded over time.

These tools aren't only helpful for reconnecting with older generations. Conversation card games offer a structured but low-pressure way to tap into the childlike traits we explored earlier, like curiosity, playfulness, and vulnerability. These are the very qualities research shows are essential to forming deep, lasting connections of any kind. Additionally, while older generations may pose unique challenges, the same principles outlined here—like asking open-ended questions, modeling emotional honesty, and taking a gradual approach—apply to siblings, partners, and extended family members who may have drifted emotionally.

Reconnecting at Work

Reconnecting with older generations often means speaking an emotional language they were never taught. In the same way, reconnecting at work requires recognizing that emotional literacy is as important in environments that don't typically make space for it. We may not use the word "emotion" in office settings, but that doesn't mean it isn't there. Emotion is always present, whether we name it or not.

We interact and form bonds and relationships with our co-workers. The health of our professional relationships impacts far more than productivity. It shapes trust, morale, collaboration, and ultimately, our capacity to lead and be led well. And when emotional literacy is missing—when we're unaware of our own triggers, when we can't manage emotional tension, or when we ignore how emotions shape behavior— miscommunication and disconnection become inevitable. People behave poorly when they're under pressure and lack the tools to navigate conflict in a healthy way.

When disconnection or unresolved tension builds at work, it doesn't stay at the office when we go home. It bleeds into the other pillars in the form of irritability, emotional exhaustion, distracted focus, or even silence with the people we care about. We carry that stress into our home relationships, into our sleep, into the way we eat, speak, and make decisions. Over time, it affects how we show up for our families, how we care for our bodies, and even whether we feel fulfilled in the life we're building.

Disconnection at work happens when people stop seeing each other beyond their roles. It shows up in strained communication, assumptions about intent, withheld feedback, or polite detachment that masks deeper frustration. Often, it emerges in situations where performance is prioritized over people—when someone feels disappointed in their own work, passed over for a role, or mistreated by a colleague. Sometimes it's not even a major event, just a conversation that went sideways or a comment that landed wrong and never got addressed.

In these moments, curiosity can be a powerful disruptor. Asking a question like, "Hey, I've been thinking about what you said; can we revisit that?" can reopen a door that would otherwise stay shut. Taking time to calmly and respectfully open communication and show you're willing to hear the other person, signals respect. On the other hand, if left unchecked, these small moments of tension can calcify into long-term disconnection.

Reconnection in the workplace means rebuilding trust, restoring clarity, and reengaging with the people you work with as fellow humans. It doesn't always require a heart-to-heart. Sometimes it's as simple as taking responsibility for how you've shown up, asking someone how they're really doing, or circling back to clear up something left unsaid.

Emotional literacy isn't the same as emotional permissiveness. Being emotionally aware doesn't mean letting go of standards or allowing poor behavior to slide. In fact, it requires strong boundaries. It means knowing how to have hard conversations with clarity and care. It means being able to acknowledge emotion without being ruled by it. Leadership at work requires both emotional fluency *and* the ability to set limits with integrity.

Reconnection in the workplace is critical for balance in the work pillar, but our sense of belonging doesn't end when we clock out. Friendships and community relationships play an equally vital role, often sitting at the intersection of self and home. These are the spaces where we express who we are outside of obligation. And like the other pillars, they require care, discernment, and emotional literacy to thrive.

Reconnection in Friendships and Community

While emotional literacy is just as important in friendships as it is at work or home, how we apply it depends on the nature of the relationship. Unlike family or workplace dynamics, which often have consistent structure or long-term commitments, friendships exist on a much wider spectrum. Some are deeply rooted and emotionally intimate. Others are more situational and based on shared activities, proximity, or a particular season of life. Reconnection doesn't look the same across all of them, and it shouldn't. Not every friendship requires hard conversations or a big emotional reveal.

That's why it's important to distinguish between the people we consider lifelong friends—those with whom we want to invest deeply—and those who are more casual connections. Since we don't invite everyone into our home or share the same stories with every person we meet, we don't need to emotionally open up in the same way with every friend or associate. But the inner work we do while developing emotional awareness, self-regulation, curiosity, and empathy will naturally start to shape the way we relate to everyone around us.

That said, in the relationships that you want to preserve or deepen, it helps to be clear about what kind of connection you're hoping to build. Reconnection may mean acknowledging a shift in behavior or expressing a desire for more meaningful engagement. Simply stating what you want your friendship to look like can open the door to a new chapter in the relationship. And don't underestimate the power of shared joy or wonder— going for a walk, watching a sunset, laughing over something ridiculous. Those moments of awe remind people why the connection matters in the first place.

Reconnecting With Emotional Literacy

Reconnection with others starts by noticing when something in a relationship isn't working as well as it could and then choosing to fix it from a place of emotional literacy. Often that disconnection stems from unspoken expectations, past disappointments, or simply the drift that happens when open communication hasn't been a priority of the relationship.

Whether it's with family, colleagues, or friends, reconnection requires us to lead with curiosity and vulnerability. It means we stop waiting for the perfect moment or the other person to go first and show up as the leaders we are, taking ownership of our own energy. At home, that might look like naming what we feel instead of retreating into silence. At work, it's about recognizing that emotional dynamics are always in play, even if no one talks about them. In community, it means understanding that not every relationship needs to be deep, but the ones that matter, deserve our extra care. Emotional literacy gives us the tools to do that: to discern, to communicate clearly, to repair, and to grow.

Now that we've learned how to rebuild trust in our relationships, it's essential to know how to receive feedback when participating in these tough conversations. In the next chapter, we'll discuss how men can receive feedback from the people in their lives and use that feedback to fuel their continued growth—without that action causing a loss of connection.

Part 3

Leadership and Legacy

Chapter 10

The Feedback Loop That Builds Powerful Leaders

*The biggest problem in communication is the illusion
that it has taken place.*
–WILLIAM H. WHYTE

The Unspoken Language of Feedback

In 1967, American psychologist Albert Mehrabian led two studies at UCLA that transformed our understanding of communication.

The first study focused on the impact of tone of voice versus the semantic meaning of words. In this context, "semantic" refers to the literal dictionary meaning of the words—the content of what is said, apart from how it is said. In the experiment, subjects listened to recorded words spoken in different tones and were asked to judge the speaker's attitude. Results showed that tone of voice was a much stronger indicator of the speaker's attitude than the actual words used.

The second study explored the relative impact of facial expressions and vocal tone. Participants were shown photos of faces displaying different emotions while listening to recorded inflections. The study found that facial expressions were more influential than vocal tone in conveying emotions.

Based on his research, Mehrabian introduced what's now known as the 7-38-55 rule: When we express feelings or attitudes, only 7% of the message comes from the actual words we use. The other 93% is nonverbal with 38% coming from our tone of voice, and 55% from our body language, like facial expressions and posture.[20] In other words, when expressing feelings or attitudes, *how* we say it and the presence we bring matters far more than *what* we say.

We are constantly receiving feedback from those around us, even when no one's speaking. A long pause, a sharp tone, a kind glance—these all communicate something. Mehrabian's research shows that most of what people communicate goes unspoken. It goes beyond performance reviews and difficult conversations, showing up in body language, eye contact, tone of voice, and even silence.

When it comes to receiving feedback, if we're only listening for formal vocal feedback, we're missing the full picture. When we start to recognize feedback in all its forms, we begin to understand that feedback is more than a performance tool. It's a core part of how we connect, grow, and lead at work, at home, and within ourselves.

---

20   Albert Mehrabian, *Silent Messages: Implicit Communication of Emotions and Attitudes* (Belmont, CA: Wadsworth Publishing, 1971).

Why Feedback Matters

Feedback, at its core, is communication. It's how we align expectations, set direction, and avoid the confusion that forms when things are left unspoken. Whether we're leading a team or running a household, feedback keeps things from falling into chaos. It provides clarity on what is expected and what needs to be improved. And it allows individuals to identify specific areas for growth and development, making it easier to take actionable steps toward improvement.

Effective feedback is also timely, meaning it should be given when it is most relevant for the person receiving it. This immediacy helps individuals make necessary adjustments in real time, enhancing their performance and interactions.

Additionally, feedback should focus on areas needing improvement but also recognize and affirm positive behaviors. This balanced approach fosters a more supportive environment, encouraging individuals to continue their good practices while also addressing shortcomings.

Feedback is a two-way process that requires active engagement from both the giver and receiver. While feedback might appear to move in one direction—from the person giving the feedback to the person receiving—it only works when both individuals are fully engaged. This is why William H. Whyte said, "The biggest problem with communication is the illusion it has taken place." As with any communication, if someone is speaking, the listener has to be receiving, processing, evaluating, questioning, challenging, and agreeing. It's an active process that requires timely engagement.

It's through this active receiving that you gain perspective on your behavior and performance, helping you identify blind spots and areas for improvement that you might otherwise miss. It's where you begin to see how others experience you—what's working, what's not, and what might be getting lost in translation. When you actively participate in the feedback process, you foster self-awareness and can then make beneficial adjustments to your approach. Feedback in this way encourages dialogue and understanding, which can strengthen relationships and enhance collaboration.

Seeking feedback demonstrates a willingness to engage in open communication. It shows that you value the opinions of others and are committed to improving your collaboration with them. By seeking feedback, you contribute to a culture of openness and constructive dialogue, which can benefit not only you but also your teams, organizations, and family members. Actively soliciting feedback reinforces a sense of commitment to personal and professional development. It signals to others that you're serious about improving your actions and that you value their input.

Ultimately, feedback is a tool for personal and professional growth. It helps individuals become more self-aware, understand how they are perceived by others, and develop the skills necessary to improve and succeed in various aspects of life. It encourages continuous learning, growth, and adaptation.

Now that we know why feedback matters, it's important to recognize that not all feedback looks the same. Feedback can take many forms—some obvious, some subtle—and understanding the types of feedback we encounter helps us respond with more clarity and intention.

Types of Feedback

Whether you're the one giving it or receiving it, feedback doesn't look the same for everyone. Each of us has a unique communication style shaped by our background, emotional state, and lived experience. Some people are comfortable with direct verbal feedback. Others prefer a softer, more nuanced approach that allows space to process. What feels helpful to one person may feel intrusive or even threatening to another, depending on timing, tone, and setting. That's why the most effective feedback is curated to the specific individuals involved.

How feedback is received depends on the emotional conditions, not only on the words used. For some, hearing feedback is a straightforward process. For others, it stirs defensiveness, discomfort, or even shame. Being mindful of this reality means we must approach feedback with humility, both when offering it and when receiving it. If you're the one receiving, humility helps you stay open long enough to understand the message beneath the words. And if you're the one giving, it helps you recognize when someone needs a different tone, pace, or environment to really hear you.

Essentially, the ability to give and receive feedback well depends on how attuned we are to the people around us. When we take the time to learn what each person needs in order to feel seen and safe, we create an environment where feedback is actually welcomed.

To better understand how feedback shows up in our lives, it helps to explore the different types we may encounter. The more fluent we become in recognizing these types, the more intentional we can be in how we offer feedback *and* how we receive it.

Formal vs. Informal Feedback

Formal feedback is structured and often occurs in designated settings, such as performance reviews, evaluations, or official meetings. It tends to follow a specific format and is usually documented. Formal feedback is typically more systematic and may involve specific criteria or standards against which performance is measured. Because it is planned in advance, it generally happens less frequently than informal feedback that arises in everyday interactions.

In contrast, informal feedback is spontaneous and occurs in everyday interactions. It can happen during casual conversations, team meetings, or even through nonverbal cues. Informal feedback is generally more immediate and can be more conversational in nature, allowing for real-time adjustments and discussions. It is often less structured and can vary widely in how it is delivered and received.

Both types of feedback are important as they serve different purposes and can complement each other in fostering communication and growth. Formal feedback provides a comprehensive assessment, while informal feedback allows for ongoing dialogue and immediate insights.

Verbal vs. Nonverbal Feedback

Verbal feedback involves spoken or written communication, including direct comments, suggestions, or critiques expressed through conversation, emails, or evaluations. Verbal feedback is explicit and allows for clear articulation of thoughts, making it easier for the recipient to understand the message being conveyed. It can be both positive and constructive, providing specific insights into performance or behavior.

In contrast, nonverbal feedback encompasses all forms of communication that don't involve words. This includes body language, facial expressions, gestures, tone of voice, and silence. Nonverbal cues can convey a wide range of emotions and reactions, often providing context or additional meaning to verbal messages. For instance, a nod or a smile can indicate agreement or approval, while crossed arms or a frown may signal disagreement or discomfort.

Both verbal and nonverbal feedback play crucial roles in productive communication. Verbal feedback provides clarity and specificity, while nonverbal feedback can enhance or contradict the spoken message, adding depth—or confusion—to the interaction. As Mehrabian's research shows, up to 93% of emotional communication comes through tone and body language, not words. That statistic alone should challenge us to pay closer attention to what's not being said. A message delivered with flat affect, distracted eyes, or closed-off posture might land very differently than intended. And if we're only listening to words, we're likely to miss the emotional truth of the message, or worse, misinterpret that message entirely.

This is where emotional literacy becomes essential. The ability to read nonverbal cues, especially in high-stakes or emotionally charged situations can make the difference between a defensive conversation and an understanding one. As leaders in our homes and workplaces, we're responsible for what we say and how we show up. Our energy speaks before we do, and if we want our feedback to build trust rather than erode it, we need to become as fluent in body language and tone as we are in language itself.

How 360-Degree Feedback Works

One model I've always appreciated is 360-degree feedback. Traditionally, this type of feedback is a tool used in professional settings to gather input from multiple sources like supervisors, peers, and direct reports. This approach provides a well-rounded view of how you're showing up.

Here's how it usually works in the workplace:

- **Multi-Source Input:** Feedback comes not only from your manager, but also peers and direct reports.
- **Self-Assessment:** You complete your own evaluation to compare your perspective with others.
- **Anonymous Surveys:** Input is often gathered anonymously, which encourages honesty and minimizes fear of repercussion.
- **Comprehensive Report:** The results are compiled to show how you're perceived by each group.
- **Development Planning:** The insights are then used to identify strengths, weaknesses, and blind spots to create a personal development plan.

What's powerful about this model is how easily it can be adapted beyond the workplace. As in an organization, each person in a family or partnership has a unique vantage point. Your partner may see one side of you, your children another, and your friends yet another. If we're only open to feedback from a narrow band of people—or only comfortable giving feedback from a position of authority—we miss out on vital insights that could help us grow.

Here's what applying this model might look like at home and with yourself:

- **Multi-Source Input at Home:** Rather than leaving feedback as something isolated at work, invite feedback from your partner, children, and close friends. Ask them simple, open questions like, "What's one way I could be a better listener?" or "Do you feel supported by me when things get hard?"

- **Self-Assessment:** As it is important at work to check in with your own perspective, a self-assessment is a crucial step in gaining feedback at home and for yourself. We've discussed different methods of self-assessment throughout the book, including journaling, mindfulness, and asking questions like, *How did I show up today? Where was I proud of myself? Where did I miss the mark?* This reflection is your personal scorecard held up against the feedback you're receiving from others.

- **Cultivate a Safe Environment:** At home, you can't really run anonymous surveys, but you can create a safe place for feedback to flourish. Remind your partner or kids that feedback is encouraged and model openness without defensiveness.

- **Honest Conversations:** Instead of a printed report, when receiving feedback at home, you gather the input over time and piece together the themes. If red flags start to pop up, such as your partner or child telling you you've been distracted lately, you know that's something that needs to be addressed and you can open honest dialogue.

- **Development Planning in Life:** Just like at work, you take what you've learned and build a plan. Maybe you decide to schedule one-on-one time with your family or to eat more nutritional food. Whichever shift you decide, the point is to turn reflection into action so you can create more balance in the home and self pillars.

Bringing a 360-degree mindset into the home encourages shared accountability and open communication. It allows feedback to move in all directions, not only from parent to child, or partner to partner, but from every member of the household. When everyone feels empowered to speak into the dynamic, we move closer to a culture of mutual respect. The result moves beyond simply improving relationships to cultivating a more emotionally honest and collaborative way of living.

Constructive vs. Affirmative Feedback

Constructive feedback focuses on identifying areas for improvement and providing specific suggestions for change. It aims to help the recipient understand what they can do differently to enhance their performance or behavior.

Constructive feedback is often direct and may highlight shortcomings but is intended to be helpful and supportive. The goal is to facilitate growth and development by addressing issues in a constructive manner.

Affirmative feedback emphasizes recognition and praise for positive behaviors and achievements. It acknowledges what the individual is doing well and reinforces those actions. Affirmative feedback is important for building confidence and motivation, as it helps individuals feel valued and appreciated. It contributes to a balanced approach to feedback by ensuring that positive contributions are also highlighted, as opposed to solely highlighting which areas need improvement.

Both types of feedback are important in fostering effective communication and personal growth. While constructive feedback helps individuals identify and address weaknesses, affirmative feedback boosts morale and encourages continued positive behavior. When we bring them together, we create a more balanced and complete conversation. That's the idea behind the old classic compliment sandwich where you layer the constructive input between affirmations and words of encouragement. In general, people tend to receive correction more openly when it's wrapped in genuine care and acknowledgment.

Self-Generated Feedback

Not all feedback has to come from someone else. Some of the most powerful insights we receive are the kind we generate ourselves through practicing self-awareness. I've found that when we take time to pause and look inward, we often already know what's working and what's not.

This kind of feedback requires intentionality. It might look like journaling at the end of a long day, noticing your emotional patterns over time, or simply asking yourself, *How did I show up in that moment? What am I proud of? What could I have done differently?*

Practices like mindfulness, meditation, journaling, exercise, device-free time, and spirituality can help you tune into your internal cues. These are the small everyday moments where we learn to check in with ourselves with no judgment and simply observe. These are the forms of introspection that lead to greater balance, credibility, and ultimately, a deeper capacity to lead.

The more we practice self-generated feedback, the less dependent we become on external validation, and the more grounded we are in our own values.

The Challenges of Giving and Receiving Feedback

Before feedback can help us grow, we have to be able to receive it—and that's not always as simple as it sounds. Some real challenges can get in the way of hearing the message clearly and responding constructively. Here's what makes receiving feedback harder than it looks.

Defensiveness: Receiving feedback can be difficult, even when we know it's necessary. One of the most common obstacles is defensiveness. If feedback is delivered in a way that feels critical or unexpected, it's easy to shut down, argue, or start justifying our actions instead of hearing the intended message. While it is a natural reaction, defensiveness prevents us from understanding how others are experiencing us, which limits your ability to grow or lead effectively.

Emotional Reactions: In addition to defense, feedback can trigger other emotional reactions, like embarrassment, annoyance, and anger; this happens especially when criticism hits close to home. Again this is normal, but it can be difficult to remain open and receptive. We need to be able to recognize these emotions without letting them run the conversation. If we get caught in the emotion, we miss the value of the input.

Misinterpretation: It's possible to misunderstand someone's tone, intent, or wording, especially when the relationship is tense or the feedback is unclear. If 93% of emotional communication comes through tone and body language, then it's easy to see how the message can get lost when we focus only on the words. That's why clarity matters—on both sides. If the feedback is vague or poorly articulated, it creates more confusion than direction. In those cases, it's our responsibility to ask questions, request examples, or get clarity on what exactly needs to change. Without that, there's no real path forward.

Fear of Vulnerability: Most people don't like being told they missed the mark, particularly when they're trying. But growth requires exposure. If we're only willing to accept feedback when it's convenient or comfortable, we're not really open to it. Part of maturity—especially in leadership—is learning to sit with feedback, even when it challenges our ego or assumptions. There is no need to agree with everything presented. But it's important to be willing to hear it, sit with it, and decide what it's saying about our impact.

Giving feedback can be just as difficult—sometimes more difficult—than receiving it. Most people aren't trained to do it well, and even those with the best intentions can get it wrong. Here are some of the challenges that can arise when giving feedback:

Timing and Setting: Feedback given in the wrong moment, such as in the heat of conflict or in public, rarely lands well. It becomes about the reaction, not the reflection. Choosing the right time and creating the right space matters. We want the person to actually hear the advice, not just defend themselves or shut down.

Balancing Constructive and Affirmative Feedback: If all we ever point out are mistakes, eventually people stop listening, and after that, they stop trying. If we only offer praise and never address what's not working, it is not doing anyone any favors. A balanced approach requires thought. We have to know what to affirm, what to challenge, and how to do both without losing the other person in the process.

Communication Style: What feels clear to us might feel abrasive to someone else. What sounds diplomatic to us might sound vague to the person across the table. That's why it's important to know our people and tailor delivery to who they are. Some people need direct, concise language. Others need space, tone, and context to take it in. It's about making the process easier and making the message land for them.

Fear of Conflict: Giving feedback can feel like inviting confrontation, especially if the relationship is already strained. But when issues aren't addressed, they build up. Over time, the absence of feedback creates more tension than the truth ever would.

Lack of Confidence: Some people don't give feedback because they're unsure of how it will land, or because they worry whether they have the "right" to say it in the first place. This lack of confidence can result in hesitance or ineffective communication. When feedback is withheld or softened to the point of vagueness, problems go unaddressed. This leads to repeated mistakes, deteriorating performance, or behavior that undermines trust. What could have been corrected early on instead becomes an even bigger issue.

When feedback is delivered ineffectively, it creates misalignment between what's expected and what's actually understood. People start filling in the blanks with assumptions, and that disconnect leads to frustration on both sides. Over time that frustration can turn into resentment since the communication did not address what needed to be said. Poor communication also chips away at trust. If people sense we're avoiding honesty or talking around the issue, they may start to question our transparency or respect for them. And ultimately, ineffective feedback creates a missed opportunity. It prevents the kind of course correction that supports growth, whether at work, in relationships, or within yourself.

Recognizing and addressing these challenges is crucial for fostering a healthy feedback culture, whether in personal relationships or professional environments. By being aware of these obstacles, we can work toward more effective communication and overall growth.

What Men Can Learn From Others

We tend to think of feedback as something that flows down from authority figures like bosses, parents, or elders. Some of the most valuable lessons can come from observing the people around us. In particular, men can learn a lot from the emotional fluency of women and the wonder, openness, and honesty of children.

Unlike men, it isn't the norm for society to pressure women to shut down their emotions in order to appear tough or capable. Because of this, women are generally seen as having a greater capacity for emotional literacy—not just being able to identify how they're feeling, but to express it appropriately, and understand how it impacts others. Studies back this up by consistently finding that women tend to score higher than men on measures of emotional intelligence, empathy, and emotion recognition.[21]

Meanwhile, cultural norms around masculinity have long encouraged men to suppress or disconnect from their emotions. Research on expressive suppression shows men are more likely to avoid expressing vulnerable emotions like sadness or shame.[22] For many men, even reaching a baseline of emotional awareness takes intentional effort.

---

21   Dana L. Joseph and Daniel A. Newman, "Emotional Intelligence: An Integrative Meta-Analysis and Cascading Model," *Journal of Applied Psychology* 95, no. 1 (2010): 54–78. https://doi.org/10.1037/a0017286.

22   Camryn Frye, "Stifled by Masculinity: A Quantitative Look at Why Men Don't Go to Therapy," *Journal of Undergraduate Research* (University of Wisconsin–La Crosse, 2022). https://www.uwlax.edu/globalassets/offices-services/urc/jur-online/pdf/2022/frye.camryn.cst.pdf.

That kind of conditioning limits our connection with others and ourselves and our ability to be effective leaders. If we can't name what's happening inside or recognize what's going on in someone else, then leadership will suffer, relationships will feel shallow, and our inner world will stay underdeveloped. Men who learn to navigate emotion with clarity and discipline become better fathers, better partners, and more grounded leaders.

If you've spent any time with children, you will have seen how kids have a natural way of approaching the world. They will come up to you with endless questions, wonder, and zero concern for whether they look foolish in the process. That openness is one of the most powerful tools for learning, and it's something a lot of men lose along the way. We start thinking it's better to look like we've got things figured out than to ask the question that would help us grow.

In his book *Fluent in Three Months*, Benny Lewis introduces an interesting line of thought that I feel is relevant to this discussion. He talks about how adults struggle to learn new languages for the simple reason that they're afraid to sound silly. Kids don't have that problem—they jump in, mess up, and try again. They apply that mindset to everything: learning to walk, making new friends, trying a new hobby like dancing, drawing, or trying a new sport. Kids know that if you can't risk being wrong, you won't grow. If you can't ask questions, you won't learn.

Men need to learn to approach situations with a willingness to explore, ask questions, and be open to new experiences without allowing the fear of appearing silly or making mistakes to control their choices. Letting go of the need to always "know" opens us to exploration, which leads to new growth.

If you watch closely, you'll see that women and children rarely move through life alone. They lean on each other, ask for help, and check in with one another. Men, on the other hand, are often taught to keep things in, handle their problems themselves, and push through the issues they face in silence. But isolation will wear down your energy, your perspective, and eventually, your relationships. There's strength in collaboration and wisdom in listening to the people around you. And there's also power in admitting that you don't have to carry everything alone.

When we pay attention to the women and children in our lives, we start to notice how much there is to learn, simply by observing how they respond to the world around them. They model a different way of being, one that can challenge us to lead with more care and a deeper understanding of what it really means to grow.

Receiving Feedback From Children

When we pay attention to those around us, we may realize that feedback often comes from unexpected sources.

For example, even when my daughter was a toddler, she provided feedback. Some of it was verbal, some of it was nonverbal, and some of it was protest oriented. Though she didn't have all the words to describe what she was feeling, she still found a way to communicate what wasn't working and what she didn't understand. Paying attention to her communication style gave me an opportunity to enhance my patience, to adjust how I listened, and to try different ways of communicating.

Adults can learn a lot from the straightforward communication and emotional honesty of children. Even young children can provide valuable insights through their reactions and behaviors that can serve as a mirror for adults to reflect on their own actions and emotional responses.

This experience with my daughter taught me as a leader that feedback doesn't always come packaged neatly. It won't always be direct or structured. In fact sometimes it's long-winded, disorganized, or emotionally charged. It may be coming from someone who doesn't speak in a professional language or isn't thinking about "constructive criticism." As leaders, part of our job is to develop the ability to listen anyway, and then to clarify, distill, and decide what's actionable.

Purposefully Seeking Feedback

When you make a habit of inviting honest input from the people around you, you gain access to perspectives you might otherwise miss. It's one of the most effective ways to identify blind spots, build self-awareness, and show others that you're serious about growth. Purposefully seeking feedback also sets the tone for open communication. It tells the people in your life—whether at home, at work, or in your inner circle—that their perspectives matter to you.

Here are a few ways to do it well:

- **Create a Safe Environment:** Make it clear that feedback is welcome. If people don't feel safe or respected, they won't speak honestly. Build trust by listening without reacting and by keeping the tone constructive.

- **Ask Specific Questions:** General questions get vague answers. Be direct. Ask things like, "What's one thing I could have done better in that conversation?" or "How did my response land with you?"

- **Choose the Right Time and Place:** Don't catch people off guard or try to force a meaningful exchange in the middle of a busy or stressful moment. Be intentional about when and where you ask.

- **Be Open and Receptive:** If you're defensive, people shut down. If you're receptive, they lean in. Make it easier for others to be honest by modeling humility yourself.

- **Follow Up:** If someone gives you feedback, circle back. Ask for clarification if you need it. Let them know what you've done with what they shared.

- **Reflect on the Feedback:** Don't rush to react. Sit with it. Ask yourself what parts of it resonate, what might be hard to hear, and what needs to change.

- **Encourage Ongoing Dialogue:** Don't make feedback a one-time event. Normalize it. Build it into your relationships so people know the door is always open.

- **Express Gratitude:** Always thank people for their feedback, even when it's hard to hear. That acknowledgment reinforces that the feedback they shared was important to you and encourages them to provide you with honest feedback in the future.

When you approach feedback with this level of intentionality, you foster clarity, connection, and real growth across every pillar of your life. One of the most powerful places to start is right at home. Sit down with the people you live with—the stakeholders in your household—and create space for real, two-way feedback. Ask them how you're showing up, and be willing to hear the answer.

While feedback is often seen solely as a professional tool, it's actually a daily practice we can invite into our lives to shape how we show up as leaders beyond the workplace, including in the home and for ourselves. Real leadership requires more than holding things together on the outside; it demands addressing the hollow man underneath, the part of you that's disconnected, emotionally shut down, or just going through the motions. In the next chapter, we'll look at what it means to restore your internal foundation so you're not just performing strength, but actually building it from the core.

Chapter 11

Restoring the Core

*The curious paradox is that when I accept myself just
as I am, then I can change.*
–CARL ROGERS

The Consequences of Emotional Neglect

We live in a world where the ability to endure without complaint is still praised as virtue. The statistics show that this silence is costing men their health, their relationships, and too often, their lives.

In 2021, the World Health Organization reported that men are twice as likely to die by suicide as women. Globally the rate is approximately 12.3 per 100,000 for men, compared to 5.6 for women. In high-income countries, where access to mental health support is greatest, the gap widens even further: roughly 3.2 men die by suicide for every 1 woman.[23] Greater access hasn't translated into greater use of mental health support.

---

23   World Health Organization, World Mental Health Report: Transforming Mental Health for All (Geneva: World Health Organization, 2022), https://www.who.int/publications/i/item/9789240110069.

Many men avoid or resist seeking help, and when they do, their struggles are often overlooked or misunderstood.

Suicide is now the third leading cause of death among young people aged 15 to 29.[24] Since 2010, suicide rates among young men have climbed by one-third. They are now higher than among middle-aged men.[25] This sharp increase underscores how disconnection and unprocessed pain are cutting into the very years that should hold the most promise.

In the United States, the crisis is even more acute. As I noted in chapter 4, men in the US are nearly four times more likely to die by suicide than women. According to the CDC, men account for nearly 80% of all suicides, despite making up half of the population. And the trajectory is rising—male suicide rates have increased by almost 25% over the past two decades, from 18.5 per 100,000 in 2002 to 23.0 in 2022.[26]

And still, most men never ask for help. In 2022 only 17% of men reported receiving mental health services, compared to 29% of women, according to a Kaiser Family Foundation (KFF) analysis of the National Health Interview Survey.[27] For most men who have ended their lives, there was no obvious warning.

24   Andrea Miranda-Mendizabal et al., "Gender Differences in Suicidal Behavior in Adolescents and Young Adults: Systematic Review and Meta-Analysis of Longitudinal Studies," *International Journal of Public Health* 64, no. 2 (2019): 265–283, https://www.ncbi.nlm.nih.gov/pmc/articles/PMC6439147/.

25   American Institute for Boys and Men. *Male Suicide: Patterns and recent trends.* Accessed August 20, 2025. https://aibm.org/research/male-suicide/.

26   Centers for Disease Control and Prevention. "Suicide Mortality in the United States, 2021."

27   Kaiser Family Foundation (KFF), "Access and Coverage for Mental Health Care: Findings from the 2022 KFF Women's Health Survey," September 27, 2023, https://www.kff.org/womens-health-policy/issue-brief/access-and-coverage-for-mental-health-care-findings-from-the-2022-kff-womens-health-survey.

Nearly 50% of people who die by suicide had no known mental health diagnosis, and many showed no observable warning signs prior to their death.[28]

There is a mental health crisis among men that is causing a hollowing out of our humanity. The statistics point to many contributing factors, but one pattern stands out to me again and again: emotional suppression. When men are denied the language, space, and tools to work through pain, it creates a chain reaction that impacts their personal health, their relationships, and their places in society.

The Consequences of Suppression

The effects of this suppression show up in the ways men try to cope.

Some try to self-soothe the discomfort caused by this hollowness with alcohol or drugs. They blur the edges of their pain in the hopes that it will pass. In the US, 12.1% of men over the age of 12 meet the criteria for an alcohol use disorder.[29] Globally, men are two to three times more likely than women to struggle with substance use disorders.[30]

---

28   Brian K. Ahmedani et al., "Health Care Contacts in the Year Before Suicide Death," *Journal of General Internal Medicine* 29, no. 6 (2014): 870–877, https://pmc. ncbi.nlm.nih.gov/articles/PMC4026491/.

29   National Institute on Alcohol Abuse and Alcoholism (NIAAA), "Alcohol Facts and Statistics," accessed August 7, 2025, https://www.niaaa.nih.gov/alcohols-effects-health/alcohol-topics/alcohol-facts-and-statistics.

30   Adrienne J. Heinz et al., "Gender Differences in Substance Use, Health, and Service Use among Veterans," Journal of Substance Abuse Treatment 85 (2018): 70–77. Also cited in: "Substance Use and Mental Health: Global Status Report," ScienceDirect, accessed August 7, 2025, https://www.sciencedirect.com/science/article/abs/pii/S0022395624002760.

Some men externalize their pain. What looks like aggression is often unprocessed grief in disguise. We see the aftermath of their behavior but rarely trace it back to its emotional root. Statistics show us that men make up over 94% of the prison population globally.[31] This figure doesn't point to a single cause, but it suggests how emotional neglect, combined with systemic factors, can turn unprocessed pain into cycles of violence and incarceration.

In the US, nearly one in nine men is projected to go to prison at some point in life.[32] Boys are often raised in environments that reward dominance over emotional awareness and that discourage emotional expression altogether. Without early intervention, those unaddressed emotional wounds metastasize. When pain isn't given a language or a means to process, it finds release in action—sometimes in ways that harm others.

Reaching out for help isn't a clear remedy to these issues in some cases. Even when men do seek help, they may struggle to articulate what they're feeling. They may also not be recognized by healthcare providers who are less familiar with how male depression or trauma presents. Mental health campaigns often miss them entirely, failing to resonate with the emotional realities men face or the way they've been taught to process pain.

---

31   United Nations Office on Drugs and Crime (UNODC), *Global Prison Trends 2024: Brief*, accessed August 7, 2025, https://www.unodc.org/documents/data-and-analysis/briefs/Prison_brief_2024.pdf.

32   Thomas P. Bonczar, *Prevalence of Imprisonment in the U.S. Population, 1974–2001*, Bureau of Justice Statistics Special Report (Washington, D.C.: U.S. Department of Justice, August 2003), https://bjs.ojp.gov/content/pub/pdf/piusp01.pdf.

It's also important to acknowledge that these challenges don't land evenly among all men. Race, culture, and community shape both the expectations of what it means to "be a man" and the resources available when support is needed. In some cultures, therapy is even more stigmatized; in others, access to care is limited or filtered through biases that leave men of color overlooked or misunderstood. The same silence that suppresses emotion for men as a whole can press down even harder depending on the cultural lens they're viewed through. The work of restoration doesn't change, but the obstacles and opportunities may look different depending on the groups we belong to.

Suicide is often the final option after all other routes have been exhausted. Long before that final decision, many men live in disconnection, managing pain they've never been taught to process. A man may appear strong and stable on the outside, but over time, disconnection, suppression, and unaddressed pain can hollow him out, leaving him fragile at the core and vulnerable, prone to collapse under pressure.

The Hollow Tree

To understand what this kind of long-term disconnection from the self does to a man, it's helpful to look at a natural pattern we often overlook until it's too late.

Trees, like men, are often seen as symbols of strength, endurance, and resilience due to their ability to withstand harsh weather conditions. From the outside, some trees appear immovable. They're tall, wide, and grounded with roots reaching deep into the earth. They've stood through storms before, sometimes for decades, seemingly unaffected. But then one day, they collapse. It's only after the fall that we realize the tree was compromised. The roots were shallow and dull, and what might have seemed a strong core was actually hollow. The tree had begun to die inside long ago—and without us noticing.

This is the metaphor I return to when I think about men in our culture.

Masculinity, as it's often taught, trains men to maintain appearances—to look steady, composed, and productive. Someone could look healthy and centered from the outside, but unbeknownst to anyone (sometimes even themselves), they are hollow on the inside. Two-thirds of men under 30 now say that "no one cares if men are okay," while one in seven claims he has no close friends.[33] Many men have been emotionally castrated by the systems that raised them, taught to sever their own sensitivity as a condition for societal belonging. The emotional suppression, the disconnection from vulnerability, and the relentless pressure to perform erodes the core of who they are. It whittles down their humanity.

When a culture celebrates this bravado type of masculinity, exalts being a "man's man," and discourages men from doing the inner work because it's seen as feminine, it creates hollow trees in the forest of our lives. From boardrooms to barbershops, this cultural mindset is hollowing out men across generations, communities, and professions. The reality is:

---

33   Daniel A. Cox, *Men's Social Circles Are Shrinking*, Survey Center on American Life, July 2021, https://www.americansurveycenter.org/why-mens-social-circles-are-shrinking/.

When you're moving around as a hollow tree, you're just one strong wind of crisis from being blown over.

The danger is, we lack the visibility to see which trees are being hollowed out faster than others. We never know what is happening inside someone else's head. Even though many men are dealing with some sort of internal decay, we don't know who might be eroding quicker because of the circumstances around them. We assume stability because we see function. But as with the tree, internal decay doesn't always present visible symptoms. It's not always clear that there are weak spots within the tree until something breaks.

Steps to Inner Restoration

So if—as I believe—most men are in some stage of hollowing out, whether it's barely begun or dangerously advanced, the question becomes: How do we start to fill what's been emptied? How do we rebuild the core before the entire structure gives way?

Before we can rebuild, we have to think critically about what's been hollowed out. For many men, it's the capacity to be sensitive, to feel deeply, to ask for help. Even something as simple as asking for directions can make us feel uncomfortable because it forces us to admit we've lost some small sense of control. This is a stereotype that holds true. What's been lost in the decay is not only function, it's the human element. It's the suppression of emotions, the inability to appear vulnerable, and the fear of seeming weak. Restoring the core is about rehumanizing every man who has had his humanity stripped away through incorrect societal expectations. That means accepting that being human is to be hurt sometimes. It's accepting that vulnerability is an expected condition of being alive.

It takes more than willpower to enact this kind of restoration. In the same way people struggling with addiction rarely heal in isolation, men navigating emotional hollowing out often need support. This is why twelve-step programs begin with acknowledgment: There *is* a problem. That same principle applies here. The hollowing out that comes from emotional suppression mirrors addiction in many ways. It isolates, numbs, and disconnects us from ourselves and from others. These steps are not about becoming a perfect version of ourselves or even performing in a better or more superior way; they're about choosing to reconnect with the parts of ourselves we have previously been taught to bury.

Restoring the core involves thinking about what is missing. The only way to rebuild is from the inside out. That is why each of the following steps addresses a different part of the internal structure: how we process pain, how we define strength, how we show up in relationships, and what we believe we're here on Earth to contribute. Let's examine what rebuilding the core requires.

Healing Inner Wounds Instead of Covering Them

A lot of the internal work that men avoid comes down to their discomfort with vulnerability. The reality is, having a wound already makes you vulnerable, whether you admit it or not. Pretending it's not there makes you more vulnerable, not less. Problems age poorly. Emotional wounds that go unaddressed compound, spread, and eventually surface in ways that are harder to manage. It's like trying to walk on a broken bone while pretending it isn't fractured. Denial makes the injury worse. There's a similar kind of denial happening when we try to act like our emotional pain isn't affecting us. The irony is that the very thing we're avoiding—acknowledging what hurts and admitting there is a problem to address—is also the first step toward becoming stronger.

Healing begins with honesty. That means identifying where we've been hurt, where we've fallen short, where something unresolved still lives in us. It means being open to getting support in the same way we'd hire a financial planner for our money or a tax specialist for our returns. When we seek help to correct our internal lives, this is the same type of wisdom we would employ in the other situations I mentioned.

The deeper issue is often a matter of real versus perceived vulnerability—how we perceive ourselves and how we fear we are being perceived by others. Many men won't admit they're struggling because they equate struggle with weakness. But it takes strength to step into the discomfort and say, "I need help." It took that same strength for me to step away and take family leave.

It wasn't something that was commonly done by other men in my organization (or in other organizations) so the choice wasn't an easy one. The same goes for starting therapy. But those decisions, as difficult as they were, put me on a healing path that's made me more resilient, not less so. Healing is the work of reinforcing the foundation—emotionally, mentally, and relationally—so the structure can hold under pressure.

This work is what allows us to strengthen the core of who we are so that we don't hollow out.

Engaging in Deep Self-Reflection

As with developing a skill in your career, building emotional insight takes repeated effort, structure, and consistency. One honest conversation, one journal entry, or one hour in therapy won't produce lasting change. Developing emotional insight has to be a consistent practice. The process of slowing down, making space, and observing what's actually going on under the surface of who you are and what choices you're making must become second nature. You can't change what you refuse to see. If you are unable to acknowledge what isn't working, there is no path forward.

That level of deep self-honesty doesn't always come easily. Sometimes we need help creating the conditions for it. For some, therapy offers the only hour in the week where they're asked real questions and are listened to without interruption. Others find reflection in coaching, men's groups, or feedback from people they live and work with. Wherever it happens, the goal is the same: to hold up a mirror and be willing to examine what you see inside of it (and underneath the surface of what you see). That includes the destructive patterns we repeat, the ways we disconnect, the emotional responses we've normalized, and the parts of ourselves we've been avoiding.

Deep self-reflection also invites us to ask better questions like:

- What part of myself have I neglected to observe and nurture in the past?
- Which emotions am I afraid to feel?

- What things in my life do I pretend don't bother me?

The answers to these kinds of questions reveal what work needs to be done.

Recovering Physiological Tools

Emotional work doesn't happen in isolation from the body. In fact, part of what hollows men out is not just emotional disconnection but also physical disconnection that can come from ignoring signals your body gives you such as suppressing stress and pushing forward even when you need rest. That's why restoration of the core also requires what I think of as the reuse of physiological tools. Breathing, stretching, movement, balanced nutrition, and particularly rest are all practices that help regulate the body and promote internal wellness. Not rest as in sleep alone, although proper sleep is important, but rest in a broader sense, taking a break from the demands of output and resetting the nervous system through small, intentional shifts.

Rest can take many forms. It might be meditation or a quiet walk. It might mean changing environments, working from a different space, or spending one-on-one time with a family member. Even simple moments of joy—laughter, music, play— can help restore the parts of us that have been flattened out by a ceaseless routine or ever-expanding responsibilities.

In his book, one I often reference, called *Rest: Why You Get More Done When You Work Less*, Alex Pang explores the many ways people can create rest in their lives. The key idea is that rest is a break from something else. It's not just about stopping. It's about choosing something that restores presence and clarity. For many men, this also means rediscovering the things that make us feel light, curious, and fully alive, in other words, restoring one's inner child. Those moments reconnect you to the parts of yourself that restore you.

Practicing Self-Compassion and Acceptance

Another vital part of restoration is practicing self-compassion and acceptance. Restoration isn't a linear journey. There will be times when old habits resurface, when the discomfort of change feels heavier than the pain you're working to heal. In those moments, self-compassion is a necessity. One of the challenges many men face is the unrelenting expectation to never have personal or professional struggles in life. We internalize the idea that any sign of emotional fatigue or confusion is a failure of character. But the truth is, restoring the inner core isn't measured by how quickly you make adjustments. It's measured by how consistently you're willing to return to the inner work.

Yet, so often, men punish themselves for not having their lives all together. They wear self-criticism like a badge of accountability, thinking it keeps them sharp. If you're going to restore what's been hollowed out, you need to lean into your full humanity. That includes grace, patience, and the understanding that struggle is part of the process. Part of that comes from learning to understand which emotions you're experiencing and which actions created those emotions.

Cultivating Emotional Literacy

At this point, emotional literacy is not a new topic to you. We've discussed how emotional literacy is the ability to recognize, name, manage your own emotions, and respond appropriately to the emotions of others. The challenge is that many men haven't been taught the emotional vocabulary required for this work. If you don't have a name for what you're feeling, it becomes nearly impossible to regulate it, let alone communicate it to someone else.

Emotions are essential to the human experience. They serve evolutionary and psychological functions. They help us recognize danger, form bonds, navigate grief, and celebrate joy. When we deny or distort certain emotions—numbing some while amplifying others—we lose the internal balance required for mental and physical well-being. Emotional suppression creates miscommunication, dysfunction, and, eventually, disconnection from our own humanity.

Beyond the internal consequences, emotional suppression can also affect the physical body. Men often die younger than women, not only because of high-risk behaviors, but because they suffer disproportionately from preventable illnesses like heart disease.[34] Stress, unresolved grief, and chronic emotional strain wear on the body over time. What we don't process emotionally, the body carries physically.

Cultivating emotional literacy begins with understanding the core emotions—things like sadness, fear, joy, anger, and surprise—and recognizing how each plays a role in a balanced, healthy internal life. These emotions are signals that give us insight, inform our decisions, and help us stay grounded in complex situations. Without emotional literacy, men often

---

34   Esteban Ortiz-Ospina and Diana Beltekian, "Why Do Women Live Longer than Men?" *Our World in Data*, last modified March 2020, https://ourworldindata.org/why-do-women-live-longer-than-men.

move through life reacting rather than responding. They default to anger or silence because those are the feelings societal influences have taught them they should feel comfortable with.

The more fluent we become in our own emotional world, the more equipped we are to engage responsibly with others. That includes learning how to support others' emotional regulation without taking on the burden of managing their responses. It means understanding that while we're not responsible for how others feel, we are responsible for how we show up—and how we avoid unnecessarily triggering or escalating situations. This level of self-awareness allows for more meaningful connection and more effective leadership. Emotional literacy gives you the ability to respond with intention, not just instinct. And in that process, it transforms emotional intelligence from a concept into a daily, relational practice.

Understanding your emotional patterns isn't only for personal insight; it's critical for leadership, parenting, and navigating complex relationships. As we've discussed, men are often socialized to regulate emotions through action rather than expression. They fix, they do, they problem-solve. But action without awareness limits growth. Emotional literacy develops through intentional practices like pausing long enough to ask yourself, *What am I actually feeling?* and *Where is this reaction coming from?* It's a process of slowing the automatic response, increasing self-awareness, and becoming more emotionally present in real time. When you become more fluent in your own experiences, you can engage more consciously, respond more thoughtfully, and lead with clarity instead of reaction. This brings us to our next vital question.

Developing a Life Beyond Performance

At a certain point in the healing process, a new question emerges: *If I'm no longer hollow and driven only by achievement, what do I live for now?* That question can feel disorienting, especially for men who've built their entire sense of worth on what they produce, solve, or achieve. For many men, the performance was about survival more than it was some arbitrary success. It was a way to feel valuable in a world that didn't offer other definitions of worth.

Developing a life beyond performance means learning to reconnect with parts of yourself that don't require validation or metrics. Rediscover passions, hobbies, or creative outlets that bring fulfillment outside of societal expectations. Joy, curiosity, play, and creativity are reminders of what it means to be fully human. This part of the work invites you to expand your identity and to recognize that you are more than what you do. Once you start to believe that, you begin to make choices aligned with the most fulfilled version of yourself. And a great way to encourage that fulfillment comes from cultivating a willingness to self-serve in addition to making personal sacrifices.

Self-Serving Without Harmful Sacrifice

Being a man, especially a father or a leader, will always involve some level of sacrifice. Making decisions that require effort, restraint, or discomfort for the benefit of others is part of the role. But there's a line between meaningful sacrifice and martyrdom. Martyrdom is when the sacrifice becomes your identity. It's when your value is tied entirely to what you give up. That kind of thinking often stems from a zero-sum mindset:

the belief that for others to win, you must lose. From a belief that there can't be mutual support, only one-way service. True leadership recognizes that growth is built on balance, which comes from multiple contributions by all the people involved

Some men only feel valuable when they're useful. They learn early that love and approval are earned through effort. Over time, they become so accustomed to giving that they forget how to receive. But support can't be a one-way street. You need the humility to listen, to admit when you've gotten something wrong, and to let others help you carry the weight. At the same time, you need the confidence to hold your own perspective, to stand firm when needed, and not default to self-sacrifice to maintain peace or avoid discomfort. Neither trait—humility or confidence—should dominate. Each must balance the other. However, these moments of balance cannot come in isolation.

Building Meaningful Vulnerable Relationships

Vulnerability is central to relationships, but for many men, vulnerability is equated with exposure. As we learned in chapter 7, real connection comes from openness. It comes from the moments when we allow ourselves to be vulnerable enough to say, "I don't have it all figured out," or "I need support." You can't build meaningful relationships while pretending to be invincible.

Building relationships on a foundation of truthful vulnerability means letting go of the relationships that reinforce emotional suppression. It means choosing people who can meet you in your full humanity. Moving beyond surface-level friendships doesn't require sharing everything with everyone. It does require the courage to be honest with the people who matter. And this brings us to the people we're making all of these decisions for—including our own selves.

Redefining Legacy: What Do You Want to Leave Behind?

Restoration isn't just about how you feel; it's about how you lead, how you relate, and ultimately, how you're remembered. The process of rebuilding your internal core isn't isolated to your private life. It shapes the way your children, your partner, your team, and your community experience you. Whether we realize it or not, we're modeling something all the time.

Legacy begins long before the end of life. It's embedded in the way we show up. It's in how we handle pressure, in how we treat people, in whether we're emotionally present or emotionally unavailable. When we commit to healing, we don't just improve our own lives, we also interrupt generational patterns. We create space for more honest relationships, more resilient families, and more grounded leadership.

As we'll explore more deeply in the next chapter, legacy is more than what you leave behind. It's who you become while you're present in your life. It all starts with the work of restoring the core.

Rebuilding Strength From Within

To put it plainly, reversing the hollowing caused by suppression requires rebuilding from the inside out. That means embracing vulnerability; practicing honest self-reflection; tending to your body's needs; cultivating emotional literacy; learning the balance of serving yourself alongside others; and choosing relationships that invite real connection. These practices fill what's been emptied and restore the core of who you are.

Restoring the core also means rehumanizing the emotional and psychological aspects that have been neglected or suppressed. It involves acknowledging vulnerabilities, healing wounds, and fostering a deeper understanding of yourself.

Rebuilding what has eroded within entails recognizing that vulnerability is a natural part of being human and that addressing one's emotional health is crucial for our overall well-being. By doing this, men can achieve a greater sense of balance and fulfillment in their lives, ultimately leading to healthier relationships with themselves and others.

Restoring the core is a lifelong practice. It's uncomfortable, often unrecognized work. But it's the kind of work that strengthens your foundation in ways performance never could.

The next chapter will explore what happens when that inner work ripples outward and how healing the core becomes the first act of redefining legacy.

Chapter 12

Building Your Legacy

*Carve your name on hearts, not tombstones. A legacy is
etched into the minds of others and the stories
they share about you.*
–Shannon L. Alder

Legacy Is a Living Practice

Most people think of legacy as something you leave behind, like a will, a trust, or a family property. Perhaps you see it as I do, as something beyond material possessions, a vestige that includes the positive influence and contribution a person makes to the lives of those who come after them. I invite you to reframe the thought that legacy is a future event—something that comes after you're gone—and see it instead as a present practice. Our most actualized legacy is rooted in the here and now, in the practices and perspectives we embody while we're still alive.

To understand legacy and why we build it, let's take a closer look at what it really means and the forms it can take.

The term legacy generally refers to something of value that is passed down from the past, often to future generations. It can include material possessions like money or property, but more broadly, it encompasses the lasting impact of one's actions, values, and influence on the world. Ultimately, legacy is about the imprint we leave on the future.

There are different forms of legacy:

- **Material legacy:** Tangible assets such as financial resources, property, inheritance, family heirlooms, or other physical items.
- **Intangible legacy:** The values, beliefs, knowledge, and wisdom we pass on; the traditions and memories we create; and the influence or inspiration we leave in our wake.
- **Living legacy:** The part of legacy we create while we're alive. Every choice and action we take today contributes to the story we are writing. Living legacy is about moving through life with purpose, making intentional decisions, and creating a positive impact in real time, not just after we're gone.

When we think of legacy this way, it becomes clear that it's not only about the end result. It's about the way we live, the example we set, and the difference we make while we still have the chance to shape that legacy.

It's like your reputation. You build it day by day, both through the choices you make and the consistency of how you show up. You can spend years building a good reputation and lose it with one poor decision. And like reputation, legacy can be damaged far more quickly than it takes to build. If your legacy becomes too imbalanced—if you're pouring all your energy into generating physical or financial provision while neglecting the emotional or mental support those you care about most need—you risk diminishing the very impact you're trying to make. People may benefit from your contributions but still carry confusion, distance, or unmet needs because they never felt emotionally supported or seen. While the accumulation of material possessions like wealth, property, and heirlooms may be part of your legacy, it also has to reflect how you engage with the world and how the world shapes you in return.

A meaningful legacy is rooted in emotional connections, knowledge, and the way individuals engage with their communities and loved ones.

True legacy involves modeling positive behaviors and practices that can inspire and guide future generations. This ultimately creates a foundation for their growth and self-actualization—the point where a person lives in alignment with their values, potential, and purpose. In this chapter, we'll explore how legacy is both a reflection of one's life and a dynamic process of influence that continues to resonate beyond one's lifetime. Let's begin by breaking down the concept of self-actualization.

The Path of Self-Actualization

Self-actualization is at the top of Maslow's hierarchy of needs. It comes after basic physiological needs, which are safety, love, and belonging. When these have been met, then esteem—achieving status, respect, and recognition—has been achieved. It's at this point where self-actualization can come into the picture. The place in life when individuals reach their full potential and find true fulfillment.

Self-actualized people are those who desire to be the most that they can be. They appreciate experiences, knowledge, and relationships more than material possessions. When one reaches this level of personal fulfillment, they realize that a meaningful life is built on understanding oneself, contributing positively to the world, and fostering connections with others.

Reaching self-actualization involves a continuous process of growth, learning, and emotional engagement, where individuals actively work towards their goals and values. It's not merely about achieving external success but about cultivating inner peace, emotional well-being, and a sense of purpose.

The important distinction to make here is that self-actualization and legacy are closely intertwined. Where we are in regards to our journey toward self-fulfillment directly influences the kind of legacy we will leave behind. When we pursue self-actualization, it shapes how we interact with others and contribute to our communities. This automatically creates a legacy that encompasses the values and lessons imparted to future generations. By living authentically and intentionally, those who reach this level of inner growth model behaviors and perspectives that can inspire others, thereby ensuring that their legacy is impactful and enduring.

In essence, self-actualization enriches one's legacy by fostering a life that is not only fulfilling for the individual but also beneficial for those around them, creating a ripple effect that can positively influence future generations.

One of the keywords I'd like you to focus on here is "fulfillment." The original meaning of fulfillment comes from the Old English *fullfyllan*, which literally meant "to fill up," as in filling a room or a ship. Over time, it evolved to mean "to carry out," "to complete," or "to bring into reality." But at its core, fulfillment has always meant bringing something to its full state, making it whole.

When we think about legacy, we often think of it as something we give away. But part of the reward of living your legacy is that it fills something in *you* too. You're not only pouring out; you're completing something. You're living in a way that feels aligned. You're not just doing more, or giving more, but *becoming* more whole in the process.

Legacy is about more than material things. You could leave your children a house to live in, and it would benefit them in a lot of ways, including supporting them on their own journeys to self-actualization (which, as leaders, should be one of our goals). But providing housing doesn't actually help in the same way as modeling practices and sharing wisdom would. As the old adage goes, "You can give a man a fish and he'll eat for a day, but teach him to fish and he'll eat for a lifetime." In other words, it's not just about what you hand off. Your legacy includes helping the people you love navigate life on their own terms.

For those who reach self-actualization, legacy becomes less about what they'll be remembered for and more about the life they're shaping right now. It's about engaging with the world in a way that changes them and the people around them. They understand that legacy isn't a monument built for the future; it's a pattern of living that others can learn from today.

With that in mind, let's take a look at how the kind of legacy you live shapes the relationships in your life.

Legacy in Relationship

The first and most important receivers of our legacy are our children. They are watching, learning, and absorbing far more than we say out loud. Our responsibility is to teach them, protect them, and meet their needs so they don't have to re-parent themselves as adults. No matter how intentional we are, they'll still have to do some healing, that's part of life. But if we model the right things, they'll have far less to repair. By showing them emotional literacy, love, and how to feel secure, we interrupt the cycle of generational trauma. We pass on more tools than wounds, making their journey to self-actualization easier.

After our children, our spouses or partners are next in line. The way we treat them becomes part of the family legacy. A relationship built on trust, respect, and emotional generosity not only sustains the partnership itself—it shapes the environment our children grow up in and influences how they will understand love for the rest of their lives. A healthy partnership also strengthens us. It's hard to model wholeness for anyone else if the relationship at the center of your life is fractured or starved of authentic connection.

From there, our legacy expands outward into our work and communities. It extends to the teams we lead, the churches we attend, and the neighborhoods we contribute to. Leadership in these spaces is part of the imprint we leave. Every interaction models the behaviors and values we want to see in the world.

The ripple effect is real. When we're intentional in these spaces, we create environments where others can thrive, and that's as much a part of our legacy as anything physical we hand down to our family.

The Legacy of Action: Every Choice Echoes

Every choice we make in our relationships, in our work, and in how we care for ourselves, creates a ripple that extends far beyond the moment. These ripples shape how people experience us today and how future generations will understand love, leadership, and responsibility.

The danger is in believing that inaction is harmless; refusing to take action is still a choice. When we neglect our own growth, avoid hard conversations, or fail to engage emotionally with others, we leave space for trauma, disconnection, and absence to take root. And trauma is contagious. Traumatic experiences often result from people who handle their emotions and situations poorly. It comes from people who may have been mistreated and who haven't figured out how to effectively re-parent themselves or how to extend the kind of loving support that others need.

Harmful patterns, whether they are shaped by emotional withdrawal, anger that turns into control, or the inability to express love, are often inherited from people who were never taught how to heal themselves. Without realizing it, we can pass on the very type of pain we once received.

That's why we face a choice. We can be conduits, carrying those damaging patterns forward, putting our own stamp on them, and passing them down to the people around us. Or we can be converters: people who stop those damaging cycles, take responsibility for what we've absorbed, and transform negative experiences into opportunities for growth. Both for ourselves and for the people around us. We can also use these experiences as opportunities to put others on the right track and help to provide them the support that helps them to live fulfilled, healthy, balanced, actualized lives. Or we could, at a minimum, help others to avoid creating scenarios that would do more damage.

The truth is, breaking these types of cycles doesn't always require grand gestures. Even small, intentional shifts—like choosing to listen instead of shutting down, apologizing when you're wrong, and showing up when it would be easier to check out—send waves that extend far beyond the moment. The smallest actions, repeated over time, can reshape an entire legacy.

Richness Is Life Forever

At some point every man has to make a choice. Do we maintain the cycles we inherited—the ones that keep us locked into harmful patterns—or do we create something better?

A big part of that choice comes down to how we define success. For a lot of us, success has been framed by what can be seen: resources, access to those resources, and the symbols that prove we have them. Usually that means money, but it can also be influence or being known and recognized by your colleagues in your field or by the wider public. Often success is thought of as the car you drive, the house you live in, the clothes you wear, or the people you're seen with.

But you can have all the money in the world and still be failing at home. You can be well-known and still be disconnected from yourself. You can have status and still be deeply unhappy. The things we can't easily display—our relationships, our health, our peace of mind—are often the truest measures of success. Your relationship with yourself will never make it to Instagram or LinkedIn, but it might be the surest path to happiness and self-actualization.

Maybe part of choosing a better future means broadening our definition of success. Success requires more than meets the eye. It all comes back to that word, fulfillment. It's about connection. It's about the quality of our relationships. It's about the generosity we've shown, the contributions we've made to other people's lives, and the sustainability of the ideas and values we've passed on.

That's why someone like Mahatma Gandhi, who owned almost nothing, could still be considered one of the most successful people in history. His success came from the influence he had on millions, the values he stood for, and the lasting change he inspired. He built movements, shaped a nation's future, and left behind principles that people still draw strength from today. His legacy is proof that the measure of a life is in what you help others become.

By the same measure, Bob Marley was once asked if he was a rich man. When the singer asked what made someone rich, the interviewer clarified, "Do you have a lot of possessions? A lot of money in the bank?" Marley laughed and said, "Possession makes you rich? I don't have that type of richness. My richness is life. Forever." He also said, "Some people are so poor, all they have is money. Live for yourself and you'll live in vain. Live for others and you'll live again."[35]

That's the kind of success worth building toward. It's not about chasing the siren call of more money, a bigger title, or your name in lights. Sometimes it's about making less so you can live more. More time. More connection. More life. That kind of success is the foundation of the legacy we leave.

The point of a legacy is to create acceleration toward a future goal so the next generation doesn't have to start from scratch. They shouldn't have to rebuild the wheel every time. They should be able to build on what we've already made—whether that's emotional literacy, healthy family patterns, community leadership, or personal integrity. That's how progress happens: not by each generation fighting the same battles over and over, but by passing down a foundation strong enough for others to stand on and push further.

A Legacy Already in Motion

When I think about legacy in my own life, my mind always goes back to the first few months after my first child was born. I had a choice: keep pushing to prove myself at work or take time away to be with my family. Choosing that time at home was the first intentional step I took in shaping my legacy. It was a deliberate decision to prioritize my role as a father and

---

35   Bob Marley, interview by George Negus, *60 Minutes Australia*, filmed in Kingston, Jamaica, 1979.

partner, to show through my actions what mattered to me most. That choice became a clear example for my family of the values I wanted to pass on: connection, commitment, and the willingness to be fully engaged in the moments that matter. While my daughter won't remember those days, that time was integral to our relationship. That choice began shaping the story she would grow up seeing, a story where love and care are at the center.

In chapter 1, I discussed how gender roles originated from practical survival needs in early human societies with men typically hunting and protecting while women nurtured and managed the home. Over time, these necessary divisions solidified into enduring cultural expectations. As a species, we've moved from mere survival (hunting, gathering, and protecting) toward creating communities, cultures, and systems that support a higher quality of life.

But civilization needs more than technology or infrastructure. If we want a future generation that is more advanced and in a better position to have quality of life and relationships, we need to continue along that path of civilization, which is inclusive of emotional literacy, compassion, and the ability to connect deeply with others. Doing that requires us to model those qualities now so our children have a foundation to build on later.

The reward of a legacy like this is not only in what we pass on but in the transformation we experience while we are living such a legacy. Each step toward emotional literacy, each moment of intentional connection, each choice to lead with compassion creates momentum. That momentum itself carries forward long after we're gone.

Legacy is not a monument carved at the end of life. It is the steady movement toward an ultimate goal, a pattern others can build on without having to start over. Each day, you're laying the foundation for someone else's next step. You're building it right now—in the way you lead, the way you love, and the way you live.

As we come to the close of this book, I hope it has helped spark awareness of where you are now, provided clarity about the gaps between who you are and who you want to be, and has delivered practical tools for building that bridge. My vision is for more men to walk in balance across the three pillars of work, home, and self, leading with strength and openness. I envision them modeling emotional literacy at home and work, while showing up for themselves as much as they do for others. Before stepping into the conclusion, take a moment to consider these questions: What does it mean to be self actualized? To be a loving parent or partner? To be a caring colleague or leader? And what does it mean to leave a legacy?

Conclusion

In 1914 Ernest Shackleton set sail on the *Endurance*, determined to lead the first crossing of the Antarctic continent. It was a mission of bold ambition, the kind of endeavor that demands both grit and glory. But the ice had its own plan. Trapped, crushed, and finally sunk by the frozen sea, the *Endurance* left Shackleton and his crew stranded hundreds of miles from civilization—in one of the most hostile environments on Earth.

At that moment, the measure of Shackleton's leadership evolved. The goal to plant a flag on new ground was forgotten as a new goal took precedence: Bring every man home alive. Over the next two years, he navigated drifting ice floes, frigid open-boat journeys, and impossible terrain. He never lost a single crew member. Shackleton's genius wasn't in conquering Antarctica. It was in knowing when to change the mission, in keeping the crew united when hope was thin, and in balancing discipline with the human connection that kept men willing to follow him into the unknown.

The same holds true for us. Life will trap and crush our best-laid plans. The pursuit of achievement will be interrupted by storms we didn't see coming. When that happens, the question will not be whether we stay the course; it will be whether we have the courage to redraw it. Whether we choose the people over the prize. Whether we lead with the steadiness, adaptability, and humanity that keep the pillars of self, home, and work standing even when the ice closes in around us.

In the end, the truest measure of legacy is not only in the peaks you stood upon as a civilized, self-actualized, loving partner or parent and caring leader, but in how many others you helped ascend toward their own highest potential because of the life you lived.

You've walked with me through every chapter, not as a spectator but as a man on the expedition willing to face the terrain, uncover the obstacles, and meet yourself as you truly are. We have questioned the roles handed down to you, dismantled the illusions you've carried, and examined the ways you've been taught to measure yourself by what you can endure rather than by who you truly are—and how to change that. This journey is not about memorizing principles. It is about reclaiming the humanity that was always yours.

What follows is not a neat recap for the sake of closure. It's a reflection of the ground we've covered. Each chapter has been a deliberate step toward restoring your balance across the three pillars—Self, Home, and Work—and toward building a life that is solid from the inside out. These extracts are reminders of what you've already proven to yourself: that vulnerability and strength can coexist, that leadership rooted in wholeness transforms everything it touches, and that the work of becoming whole does not end here. This is the beginning of your next chapter. Now, let's take a look at the journey we've traveled together throughout these pages.

- **Chapter 1 – The Making of Men:** You have inherited scripts about manhood that were born from ancient necessity but now often work against the life you truly want. This chapter explored how redefining strength means moving beyond outdated expectations to lead with balance across self, home, and work—grounded in emotional awareness, purpose, and growth.

- **Chapter 2 – The Disconnected Man:** Disconnection is the thief of a man's humanity, convincing him to overfeed his work while starving both his self and home. Here, you learned that reclaiming wholeness begins when you challenge fear-based definitions of power, embrace vulnerability as strength, and take full responsibility for reparenting yourself so presence, purpose, and leadership can coexist in all three pillars of your life.

- **Chapter 3 – Success at the Expense of the Self:** Real success is not measured by constant competition, status, or the single pillar you've overdeveloped, but by the balance you create across self, home, and work. This kind of success is about aligning your inner values with outer actions so that achievement is sustained by presence, peace, and purpose rather than driven by fear, comparison, or performance alone.

- **Chapter 4 – The Three Problems That Stand Between You and Wholeness:** The three core problems—trading wholeness for performance, suppressing emotion, and clinging to control—are cultural patterns that erode connection, balance, and fulfillment. But by naming and confronting these issues now, men can disrupt the destructive cycles these problems create and realign the three pillars of self, home, and work, and live without the deep regrets that come from misalignment.

- **Chapter 5 – Servant Leadership Across the Three Pillars:** Embracing servant leadership across the three pillars means leading with empathy, integrity, and a commitment to others' growth in every role you occupy. This creates balance both between and within pillars so that who you are privately, relationally, and professionally aligns with your values and fosters lasting impact.

- **Chapter 6 – The Art of Wobbling Well:** In this chapter, you learned that balance isn't a fixed state but the ongoing skill of "wobbling well"—making small, intentional adjustments across pillars, staying responsive to change, and recognizing that imbalance in one pillar ripples into the others. So the goal is not perfection but sustained alignment over time.

- **Chapter 7 – Practicing Emotional Leadership:** Emotional leadership replaces the old dominance model with a balance of warmth, competence, and vulnerability. In this chapter, we learned that choosing authenticity over performance, redefining protection to include emotional availability, and leading in a way that builds trust, deepens connection—combined, these actions will sustain our inner selves and those we serve.

- **Chapter 8 – Reconnecting With Oneself:** Reconnecting with yourself means closing the gap between who you truly are and the roles, expectations, and inherited standards of living. By releasing harsh self-judgment, reshaping your inner voice with compassion, and choosing alignment over performance, every relationship we touch benefits from the empathy and authenticity we've reclaimed.

- **Chapter 9 – Reconnecting With Others:** Reconnecting with others begins with recognizing where trust, vulnerability, and emotional presence have eroded, then choosing to restore them using emotional literacy. We want to show up with curiosity, openness, and care across family, work, and community so that our relationships not only survive but actively deepen and strengthen the other pillars of our lives.

- **Chapter 10 – The Feedback Loop That Builds Powerful Leaders:** This chapter explored how feedback is more than a performance tool; it's a continuous, two-way process that, when approached with emotional literacy, curiosity, and humility, strengthens trust, sharpens self-awareness, and fuels growth across every pillar of life.

- **Chapter 11 – Restoring the Core:** We examined how to reverse the hollowing caused by emotional suppression—rebuilding from the inside out through vulnerability, self-reflection, physiological care, emotional literacy, balanced self-serving, and meaningful relationships—so we can live, lead, and leave a legacy from a place of wholeness rather than performance.

- **Chapter 12 – Legacy:** Finally, we discussed how legacy is not a distant event that happens after we die, but a present, daily practice of self-actualization. It's built by living in a fulfilling way that models emotional literacy and creates a foundation others can build upon. When we live this way, our impact is measured not just by what we leave behind, but by how we lead, love, and live right now.

This is where our work together ends, at least within the pages of this book. But your personal work and development continues. The conversations we've started here are meant to live on in the way you lead yourself and others.

If you want to keep building on what you've learned, I invite you to join me beyond this book. Visit www. ExecutiveParentCompany.com to be the first to know about future book releases, find new resources, discover deeper explorations of the Three Pillars, and gain access to *Executive Dad* podcast, where we continue to challenge the outdated definitions of masculinity, leadership, and legacy. You'll also find ways to work with me directly—through executive coaching, speaking engagements, and other opportunities designed to help you grow in alignment with your values.

And if you'd like to reach out personally, you can contact me at kenyada@executiveparentcompany.com. The book may be finished, but the journey toward becoming your fullest self is just beginning.

Acknowledgments

This book was born from the conviction that strength and sensitivity are not opposites, but partners in power. It also stems from an uneasy, personal journey that has approached vulnerability and weakness head on in the pursuit of real fulfillment and contribution. The New Alpha is the culmination of countless conversations, reflections, and experiences shared with leaders, fathers, sons, and friends—as well as all the important women in my life—who have taught me what balance truly means.

I am deeply grateful to my family whose patience, love, and honesty have grounded me and influenced every word written here. To my mentors and colleagues across boardrooms, classrooms, cities and countries—thank you for showing me that integrity and intellect can coexist with empathy and grace. They also require tenacity and resilience.

Special thanks to the thinkers and doers including those at Harvard Business School who were and have been there for me as I clarified my purpose. These are the men and women redefining and reshaping leadership in their own ways. Together, with courage and consistency, we can indeed change the world.

Finally, to the readers who dare to become New Alphas: May this book serve as both a mirror and map, guiding you toward the power that balances and beautifies rather than dominates, that heals and helps rather than harms, that drives deep humility as the foundation of confidence and progress.

About the Author

Kenyada Meadows is a global finance executive, author, and founder of The Executive Parent Company, an ecosystem devoted to helping high-performing professionals lead with balance across three pillars—their relationships at work, home, and with themselves. Kenyada has also authored the poetry collection, *Afloat, Atop a Marbled Sea*, which can be found in book stores everywhere.

Drawing from decades of leadership experience at Fortune 25 institutions and his own evolution as a father, thought leader, and entrepreneur, Kenyada developed The New Alpha framework. This framework redefines strength and success not through dominance, but through emotional intelligence, humility, and balance across life's domains.

His connection to the topic is deeply personal and he has discovered what drives and supports true power. He wrote this book to share that with you.

www.ingramcontent.com/pod-product-compliance
Lightning Source LLC
Chambersburg PA
CBHW071731120626
46550CB00002B/483